Soccer iQ Presents
Shutout Pizza
Smarter Soccer Defending for Players and Coaches

BY DAN BLANK

ISBN: 0989697762
ISBN 13: 9780989697767

If you'd like to order this book in bulk at a discounted rate,
please email me at coach@soccerpoet.com

For a free PDF of more defending exercises that complement this book,
please visit www.soccerpoet.com.

I hope you'll be my Twitter friend: @SoccerPoet.

This book is dedicated in loving memory to Paul 'Ace' Hayward, a fantastic coach and better person.

Paul Hayward
March 3, 1959 –
February 26, 2015

His entire existence was predicated on the solitary principle of making other people happier than they were ten seconds ago.

Please help spread Ace's legacy of kindness –
and support his son's financial future – by purchasing a t-shirt at:

http://saltybrands.com/collections/hayward-von-max

and

http://11mangang.com/11ManGang/Products

TABLE OF CONTENTS

RISK MANAGEMENT IN POSSESSION 155

DEFENDING SET PIECES 173

SITUATIONAL DEFENDING 187

INTRODUCTION

In 2009, after two seasons as a volunteer coach, I was promoted to full-time status and assumed the role of defensive coordinator at Ole Miss. The team had come off two straight losing seasons and it had been made clear that if we didn't reach the NCAA Tournament, our staff would no longer be coaching at Ole Miss.

The star of our back four was a rising senior named Danielle Johnson. I could sing Danielle's praises for days on end, so let me just summarize by saying she is arguably the best player I've ever coached. In addition to being our best defender, Danielle was also one of our most talented attackers. A week before preseason, my boss, Steve Holeman, decided to convert her into an attacking midfielder. It wasn't great news for the guy charged with organizing our defense, but I wholeheartedly supported Steve's no-bullets-left-in-the-chamber gamble. If we were going to lose our jobs, we wouldn't do it with our best attacker stuck at center back.

With or without Danielle, my first decision was to make a pretty substantial overhaul of our approach to defending as a back four. It was an ambitious undertaking because my views on defending were very different from my predecessor's. First and foremost, I planned on teaching the defenders to think the game differently, and that meant I needed every teaching tool I could get my hands on.

If you think you can just make a coaching point to a group of players and expect that all of them will understand it, digest it and recall it at the proper moment, you're going to be in for a lot of disappointments. I've always believed that if you want players to understand what you're teaching, then you have to spell it out for them. So that's what I decided to do. I typed out everything I could think of as to how our back four would operate, drew up some diagrams, ran the file down to Office Depot and had them assemble it into a spiral-bound book. I bought enough copies for each defender and handed them out on the first day of preseason. The book was simply called *How We Defend*.

How We Defend was the foundation of our defensive scheme. It outlined the core philosophies that would govern our actions and presented the defenders with the solutions to different puzzles they would encounter on the field. It wasn't everything, but it complemented what we were doing on the field and what we would be watching on video. It was one more way to help the players internalize the information I was providing, and that's all the justification any coach will ever need.

That season our starting back four consisted of one senior, one sophomore and two freshmen. Our goalkeeper was a 5'6" sophomore walk-on. We were young, inexperienced, missing Danielle Johnson and learning a whole new approach to defending. And we ended up with the lowest goals-against average in the SEC, the team's first winning season since 2006 and a trip to the NCAA Tournament.

In the spring of 2010, I followed my boss to the University of Georgia where I would inherit a new batch of defenders. To my delight, one of those defenders, Laura Eddy, had just been named the SEC's Freshman of the year. And just as he had done to me at Ole Miss with Danielle, Steve kidnapped my extremely talented center back and converted her into a midfielder. Once again, it didn't matter.

Using the same principles and the same handbook, albeit with a different logo on the cover, UGA led the SEC in goals-against average.

Were those back-to-back years of leading the SEC's best defense the result of a handbook? No way! At least not entirely. Both universities were blessed with talented players – defenders and attackers – and in the top tier of college soccer, you're not winning without talent. The book, however, helped unite those defenders to a single governing philosophy. It helped each player understand her role and her positioning and it helped her prioritize her decisions when faced with a litany of choices. And it helped each player understand the roles of each of her teammates. In short, *How We Defend* got everyone on the same page. Literally.

This book is a vastly expanded, more detailed version of *How We Defend*. It also includes some chapters from *Soccer iQ Volumes 1 & 2* that focused on defending. I hate to recycle content, but a book on defending would be hopelessly incomplete without those chapters.

This book focuses primarily on the organization of a back four and doesn't delve very deeply into the goalkeeper's role as a part of the defensive unit. Believe me, I understand that the goalkeeper's role goes far beyond stopping shots. If you're looking for a book that focuses on this aspect of goalkeeping, this isn't the right book for you. Just put it down and walk away.

By that same token, this book isn't a collection of drills. You'll find some drills scattered throughout, but most of the diagrams lean towards defensive organization. However, I have put together a PDF companion book of defensive drills that you can download for free from www.soccerpoet.com. It's my gift to you.

I wrote this book to help players and coaches. A lot of those coaches won't agree with some of my philosophies and you may be one of them. That's fine. Soccer would be very boring if every coach shared a single ideology. All I'm saying is that this is what worked for us and that it might work for you too. I hope you enjoy it and find it useful.

SHUTOUT PIZZA

1

Shutout Pizza

I t was a Wednesday night. While most of their teammates were meeting with tutors or socializing with friends, the defenders and I were gathered in the video room at the soccer complex, making small talk and laughing… and eating. A few minutes later we would be reviewing the video of our weekend performances. Each week I would produce two DVDs – one with clips from our Friday night match and one with clips from our Sunday match. Each DVD was about six minutes long, but with the amount of pausing incorporated to discuss specific moments on each video, the session would last roughly 45 minutes.

One of the governing tenets of our defense was that it was our job to give our team a chance to win. That meant keeping the ball out of our net. To that end, it had been a great weekend. We had recorded a weekend sweep with two non-conference wins. Better still, we hadn't conceded a goal. The results ran our shutout streak to six straight games. Still, as an old friend once told me, you don't have to be sick to get better. In this room is where we would get better.

We would dissect the most important and teachable moments from each match – things we did well, and things we needed to improve upon. We would tackle things as large as team shape and as small as the proper positioning of someone's lead foot. We might critically examine a player whose hips were turned the wrong way then, moments later, celebrate her courage for standing in the way of an opponent's shot.

Each player's every movement was a candidate for the big screen. There was nowhere to hide in this room... certainly not on Wednesday nights. Each defender dreaded those moments when it might be her turn... when the screen froze on her and a group discussion commenced on where she should have been or what she should have done differently. But with each passing week those moments became less anxiety-ridden, as the players began to make peace with the fact that everything we did here was to make everyone better.

I relied on video as an invaluable teaching tool in the development of our defenders, both individually and as a unit. When we turned down the lights, we would delve into both the big moments and also the minutia, the goal being that we were better in our next game than we were in our last one. We knew that in our sport, perfection was unattainable. We would never be perfect, so we would have to settle for being impenetrable. My objective was that each player not only understood her position, but the position of every other player in our back four. I wanted each player to know where each of her teammates was, where they should be, and why. And I wanted them to understand the details and why they were important.

Whereas successful attacking is often the result of an individual moment of brilliance, successful defending is more of a ballet that requires precise synchronicity amongst all members. That's why I might call out a player for being a half-step too wide, even if she was fifty yards from the ball and even if nothing came from it. It was during these video sessions where the players grew accustomed to hearing one of my favorite sayings: *Just because you got away with it, that don't make it right.* It was all about the details.

Regardless, we'd had a very good weekend. So, as was tradition on the Wednesday after a shutout, before we dove into the video critique, we shared a couple of pizzas from Peppino's, a small but outstanding pizza joint just down the road from our stadium. The score of each game was Sharpied onto the box lids. It was how we celebrated our lockdown performances. More importantly, in a world that celebrates attackers and often neglects defenders, those pizzas were a trophy for the grinders who gave our team a chance to win. We called it Shutout Pizza.

2

The Team within the Team

We had just taken a three-goal lead on an opponent we were utterly dominating. There were still 25 minutes left to play, but the result was in the bank. My boss, Steve Holeman, began resting our starting group of attackers, trying to protect them from injury and preserve their legs for our next game. Our reserves shouldn't have a problem seeing out the game. But there was still one more order of business to attend to.

I knew the question was coming and I was dreading its arrival. Steve knew what my answer would be, but that never stopped him from asking. Over the past six years, this became a sort of Abbott and Costello routine between the two of us. Steve asked if I wanted to make any changes in the back four. It was more of a hint than a question.

"Nope," I said.

"Are you sure?"

"Yep."

"This might be the only chance that so-and-so gets for the rest of the season," he countered.

"Too bad."

And we'd go round and round like this until one of us eventually caved.

Whenever we had a comfortable lead, Steve wanted to reward those players who came to training every day but hardly ever got to step on the field during a game. As you can see, I wasn't as magnanimous.

Our defenders took great pride in shutouts. When the game was over and the media guys with the cameras and notebooks strolled onto the field, they were going to interview the players who scored the goals. The attackers provided the goals and the goals provided the sizzle. The defenders would walk off the field, straight past the reporters who had no interest in hearing from them. That's not a pity party; that's just life as a defender.

In 2013 we had a run of six straight shutouts. During that stretch, the only member of the defensive unit who was asked for an interview was the goalkeeper, and that was after the sixth game. Again, life as a defender.

Steve is a lifelong attacker – an extremely talented one – who even captained Wake Forest to an ACC Tournament championship. He sees the game through an attacker's eyes. I was a forward/midfielder who was converted to defender when I got to college, so I see the game through a different lens.

As a forward, I was happy if we won and even happier if I happened to score in that win. If we won 5-4 and I scored a goal, I was elated. But everything changed when I became a defender. If we were winning 3-0 and gave up a goal to finish 3-1, I was pissed. I was pissed that we couldn't close the deal. I doubt that any of our forwards walked off the field distraught that we won 3-1, and therein lies the rub: *Defenders are not forwards*. Defenders have a different measuring stick, and as such, I believe you should tailor your approach as to how you coach them.

How We Defend offered almost nothing in terms of psychology, but I've always believed in making the defensive unit – the defenders and goalkeeper – a team within the team. I looked for ways to bond them as a unit because that's the only way they would succeed – as a unit. That's why we had Wednesday night video sessions and separate pre-game meetings and happily, Shutout Pizza. That's why, at training, when we would run the attackers against the defenders, I would use drills like the *Impossible Game*, an exercise you'll read about later. I looked for any opportunity to drive them closer together, whether through shared misery or shared celebration.

All units need something tangible to drive them, and for our defenders, a shutout was our tangible objective. Don't get me wrong; they appreciated and celebrated every win, but looking up at the scoreboard at the end of the game and seeing a zero in the opponent's column was the ultimate prize. And when that prize was within arm's reach, it was demoralizing to let it slip away, especially if they felt the coaching staff was the lead saboteur.

I didn't enjoy those moments when we made wholesale changes in our front six because it invited more pressure from the opponent. I wanted the defenders to get their shutouts and every starter we pulled off the field improved the opponent's chance to score. I'm not silly enough to think that shutouts are solely the result of the back four or the goalkeeper. The players in front of them have a tremendous say in how busy our defenders will be, so I preferred keeping our best players on the field to protect our defense. However, I also knew the importance of saving the legs of our attacking players, so I didn't protest the changes to our front six. But when it came to the defenders themselves, I was steadfastly opposed to making any unnecessary changes. So Steve and I would have our debates.

I am an ardent believer in the idea that a team's pride comes from its defense. Let me run a hypothetical by you: Would you take more pride in robbing someone else's house or in protecting your own? Yes, maybe if we lived in a lawless society, you might get a certain sense of misappropriated power from going into someone's home and helping yourself to the safe and the Samsung, but wouldn't you feel prouder of protecting your home and your family from an intruder who tried doing the same to you? Of course you would!

It's no different in soccer. Even if they don't realize it on a conscious level, teams internalize a sense of pride when they leave the field knowing they kept their house safe from an opponent that spent 90 minutes trying to break in. It's especially important for defenders because protecting the house is their primary responsibility. With every shutout, their pride grows, their loyalty to the cause grows, and their confidence grows. These are all good things.

My advice is to stop treating your back four like they are just four more players on your team and start treating them as a unit — as a team within the team. To reach their potential, your defenders have to work as a unit and they have to want to play for one another. You won't get that from them unless you see the game through their eyes too.

3

Details

As a college coach, I had the luxury of working with my defenders almost every day, especially during the fall. During a typical training session, we would split the attackers from the defenders and I would train the defenders for thirty minutes before we reconvened as a team. You may not enjoy that same luxury and that makes your job more difficult than mine. Because we spent so much time together, we had the opportunity to cover some of the most minute details you could ever imagine. For example...

I decided to devote ten minutes of one session to a very specific situation in which the ball was popped up in the six-yard box and the defender, facing her own goal, had to head the ball over the crossbar. How often have you seen that happen? Rarely, right? Still, we had the time so I figured I would introduce the topic just in case the moment ever presented itself. Sure enough, a few weeks later, we were playing Alabama and the ball floated into our six-yard box and over our goalkeeper. Our left back, Nikki Hill, from three yards in front of the goal, calmly nodded the ball over the bar, conceding a corner kick instead of a goal. It was one of those critical moments that will never appear in the statistics, but it saved the game.

My point is this: Details matter.

If you want your back four to realize their potential, you can't just tell them their positions and throw them onto the field and hope for the best. You've got to coach every bit of their game, just as you would with your attacking players, and you can't settle for anything less than excellence. If a forward uses poor technique and her shot sails over the bar, your team misses out on a great opportunity and everyone knows it. In that sense, your forward doesn't get away with it. Then maybe the next day you'll work with her on keeping her toe pointed down when she strikes the ball so she doesn't make the same mistake the next time around. Defenders, on the other hand, will get away with an astonishing amount of imperfections… *if you let them.* If you only coach your defenders when their mistakes get punished – as in, when the other team scores or nearly scores – then you're inviting disaster.

When you coach attackers, then presumably, an attacker has the ball. Imperfections are immediately noticeable. For our purposes, when you coach defenders, you're coaching players who don't have the ball. That means you have to focus on things like their decision-making, their positioning and their stance. And those are easy things to overlook when the ball doesn't end up in your net.

Remember this: When you let your defenders get away with the little things that didn't scorch you in the here and now, you're enabling bad habits. And those bad habits will most certainly resurface to bite you in the butt. As I already mentioned (and forgive my neighborhood grammar), just because you got away with it, that don't make it right.

Defending excellence is found in the details. The more time you spend focusing on them, the better prepared your defense will be.

4

The Object of Defending

When the other team has the ball, what's the most important thing?

Ask that question to your team and I'll bet that nearly 100% of them will give you this answer: *Get the ball back.*

From *How We Defend*:

> The opponent gains possession of the ball. Until we get the ball back, the only thing that matters is that *they do not score.*
>
> THEY DO NOT SCORE.
>
> All of your decisions must be governed by this one premise. It's *not* about taking the ball from them. It's about keeping it out of our net.

Defenders constantly must choose the lesser of two or more evils, such as:

- Do you retreat 1v1 or do you tackle?
- Do you keep your feet or do you slide to block a cross?
- Do you mark tight on a player or do you leave her so you can support the first defender?

Defending is constantly about choosing the least in a series of evils. But in the end the only thing that really matters is that we make it as difficult as humanly possible for them to score. So whether you are the first defender or the third defender, *every decision you make must ultimately be governed by doing the thing that makes it the most difficult for the opponent to score.*

When asked, "What's the most important thing when the opponent has the ball," most players will say, "Get the ball back."

No! No, no, no!

We will get the ball back. Sooner or later, we'll get it back. But if your #1 priority is to get the ball back, you will play with impatience. You will pull us out of our shape. You will make a mistake that will start a domino effect that will undo us.

Getting the ball back is a means to an end. Getting the ball back is a tool to keep them from scoring. When you confuse these two, you cause us problems. *If they are not scoring, they are not hurting us.*

Getting the ball back is important, but it is not as important as NOT letting them score. Their possession doesn't hurt us. Their scoring kills us. Remember that!

Remember our #1 priority: THEY DON'T SCORE! It is the backbone of everything we do.

We will be aggressive. We will chase and we will hit. We will pressure relentlessly. But we will be smart about it.

Not letting them score... that is our job. Above all else – THEY DON'T SCORE.

The ultimate objective of defending is to keep the ball out of your net. If your defenders answer incorrectly to the question at the start of the chapter, then they don't know their purpose. It's impossible for players to reach their potential if they don't understand the very purpose of their job.

Defenders are constantly making decisions, constantly trying to choose the least in a series of evils. When they fully understand the objective, they are better at prioritizing their decisions. They can more quickly filter through the list of alternatives and get to the one that is ultimately the correct one: *What can I do that will make it the most difficult for them to score?*

It doesn't matter if it's the first defender in a 1v1 situation or the weak-side defender in a 6v6; every decision and every movement should be governed by the idea that the opponent doesn't score. This is a theme we're going to hammer away at, so get used to it.

When defenders internalize this premise, you'll see it. You'll see them putting more thought into their decisions and better managing their risks; you'll see them talk themselves out of a foolish challenge; you'll see them make corrections in their decision-making. And you'll see that you're conceding fewer goals.

5

Principles

I believe that there are certain inalienable principles to defending and that these principles never waiver. If your players can stay true to these principles, it will be very difficult for teams to score against you.

From *How We Defend*:

They DO NOT Score – That is Priority #1

How do we keep them from scoring?

- Get numbers behind the ball.
- Protect the space behind our Back Four.
- We defend the goal, not the sidelines.
- Always, always ALWAYS protect the center.
- The ball does not penetrate between defenders. NO SPLITS!
- Give them sideways and backwards, but ALWAYS protect the goal.
- Get inside of their attacking shape.

- Defend in numbers. Hunt in packs.
- Recognize when she is or is not dangerous.
- Recognize when she is or is not in shooting range.
- Getting the job done is more important than *who* gets the job done.

Those principles were the foundation for our defense. Let's review them one at a time.

Get Numbers Behind the Ball

The bigger the crowd that the opponent has to play through, the less likely they are to score. Bigger numbers favor the defending team; smaller numbers favor the attackers. For example, 2v2 is a much more dangerous attacking equation than 5v5 even though the teams are numerically even in both examples. The more bodies involved in the fray, the more difficult it becomes for the attacking team.

When the opponent gains possession of the ball, the defenders must work to get between the ball and the goal to start forming that crowd. There are a zillion different scenarios a defender will face, but you can't go wrong by getting your body between the ball and your goal.

Protect the Space Behind Our Back Four

Particularly when your defenders are pushed high up the field, there develops a no-man's land in front of your goalkeeper and behind your defenders. When the opponent takes possession of the ball, this no-man's land is where you are most vulnerable. Recognizing and reacting to this situation is pivotal when it comes to protecting your goal. We'll cover this topic in greater detail in a later chapter.

We Defend the Goal, Not the Sidelines

Some coaches prefer funneling the attacking team toward the middle of the field. I am not one of them. I'm not saying my choice is inherently better; I'm just saying this is my preference for the simple reason that the goal is in the center of the field and I prefer that the ball be angled away from the very thing we are trying to protect.

Your defense can't take away everything. If you defend the forward pass, you concede the negative pass. If you take away the right side, you concede the left. Our objective was to always defend the goal at the price of conceding the sidelines.

This concept is critical in the individual decisions that defenders make about their positioning off the ball, the opponents they choose to mark, the spaces they choose to occupy, and their angle of approach as the first defender. Remember, defending is always about choosing the least in a series of evils.

For now let me oversimplify: If the opposing center midfielder has the ball 35 yards out from our goal and has the choice of successfully passing the ball to the center forward or to the right wing, we want that ball going to the right wing.

We wanted to build a force field in front of our goal – a bubble if you will – and force the opponent to play wide of that bubble.

This same concept applies to positioning off the ball. If the weak-side defender has to choose between marking a forward who is in front of our goal or a forward who is wide of it, we want her marking the player in front of our goal. As obvious as this sounds, a defender will commonly choose to mark 'her player' instead of figuring out who the most dangerous attacker is and making the adjustment.

Always, Always, ALWAYS Protect the Center

Remember in the introduction when I said you need to spell things out? Well, this is just another way of spelling out that we defend the goal and not the sidelines. When defenders don't know how to prioritize, they try taking away everything. When they do that, your team is more vulnerable. Defenders must be willing to concede wide play in order to protect what's important. We were going to defend from the inside out at all costs.

Again, I know this sounds obvious, but I'm talking about a lot of split-second decisions and position corrections that are sometimes no more than half-a-step.

The Ball Does Not Penetrate Between Defenders

The most dangerous forward passes are ones that split a pair of defenders. We refer to this pass as a *seam ball* or a *split*. It is critical that defenders understand how to take up a shape that prevents these passes from penetrating. This is going to rely heavily on the second and third defenders taking up positions that close the seams to either side of the first defender.

If we are going to protect the center, we must be phenomenal at taking away forward passing seams. You can't accomplish one without also accomplishing the other. Eliminating seam balls is a topic we'll revisit throughout the book.

Give Them Sideways and Backwards but Always Protect the Goal

Okay, it's the third way to say the same thing. Defenders need to know that it's okay to concede some of the opponent's actions. Failure to concede a negative pass will often come at the expense of conceding a forward one. Failure to concede a pass to a winger's feet can result in a pass that splits the defense. Protecting the goal is Priority #1 and there aren't enough ways to get that point across.

Get Inside of Their Attacking Shape

This is another element of protecting the middle, but now we are often talking about the positioning of the weak-side defender. The width of the opponent's attacking shape is determined by their widest players who are within, or close to, shooting range, prioritized by those attackers who are closest to the goal. One thing I'll tell an outside back is that if she looks to the sideline and doesn't see an opponent between her and the sideline, then she is too wide.

I prefer my weak-side outside backs to pinch way in toward the center of the park, even if the attackers in that area are already marked. This allows her to help the central defenders because they are the ones dealing with the attackers in the most threatening positions. If a ball skips past the center back or she gets turned by the forward, the outside back needs to be in a position to help. The objective is to protect the middle and adjust to the outside.

Biggest Threat

In this diagram, the right back is inside of the opposing left midfielder but wide of the left wing. This is bad positioning because the winger is the more immediate threat. The outside back should be positioned inside of the winger to deal with the most dangerous threat. She can adjust if the ball is played to the outside midfielder.

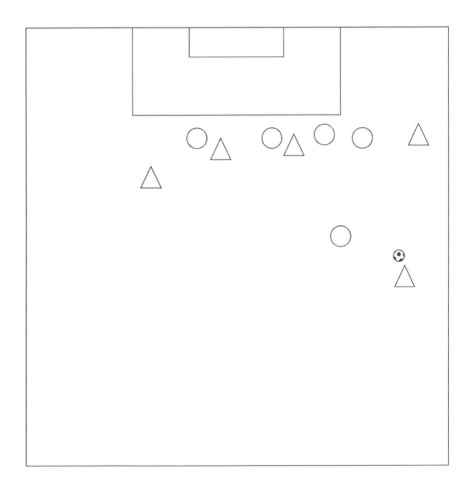

Defend in Numbers, Hunt in Packs

One of the great mistakes of defenders is an eagerness to engage in 1v1 battles, particularly when they don't have cover from a second defender. When the opponent is advancing the ball, your defenders should be consolidating. They should be working to get behind the ball and also to reduce the space between one defender and the next. We aren't looking for a fair fight. We are looking for an unfair one! Why engage an attacker 1v1 when, if you delay for three more seconds, you can force that attacker into a 1v2? Defenders should always be looking for ways to stack the deck in their favor, and the best way to do that is to create situations where you outnumber the attackers. This is a theme we'll revisit throughout this book.

Recognize When She Is or Is Not Dangerous

Many of a defender's decisions should be based on whether or not the opposing player is dangerous, and there are varying degrees of danger. For example, the further your opponent is from the ball, the looser you can be to her. The further she is away from your goal, again, the looser you can be to her. An opponent on the ball is a lot less dangerous from midfield than she is from your 18. Recognizing an opponent's threat level and adjusting accordingly is a hallmark for smart defending.

Recognize When She Is or Is Not in Shooting Range

There is no greater danger than a player on the ball within shooting range of the goal. We're going to talk a lot about retreating when the opponent is running at us with the ball, but eventually there comes a time when you have to stop retreating and make a stand. At that point, the role of the first defender is to either make a tackle or block a shot.

It's important to have a clearly defined idea of what qualifies as shooting range. As a coach of college women's soccer, I set that line at two yards in front of our 'D.' Can players shoot from further out? Absolutely. Do they? Rarely with accuracy, but even in retreat, we still need to concern ourselves with a potential shot from beyond our designated shooting range. It's not like we just run toward our own goal and then wait for the attacker to arrive. While retreating, the first defender should be making constant adjustments to deter and/or get in the way of a potential shot.

When the defenders are in retreat mode because an opponent is dribbling up the gut, they need to have their proper shape configured before the attacking player gets to shooting range. Knowing that gives them incentive to work hard at the right time. We'll cover this in more detail in a later chapter.

Getting the Job Done is More Important Than 'Who' Gets the Job Done
Too often a defender will confuse *her* job for *the job*. The opponent will score and this defender will say, "It wasn't my fault; I had *my* man." The job – protecting the goal – is everyone's responsibility. Don't think that your job ends with tightly marking *your player*. Defending requires the ability to read the situation and make adjustments, even if that means leaving *your* man. When the goal is threatened, it's all hands on deck! Tightly marking your man doesn't do the team any good if there is a more dangerous threat at hand. If your services are required elsewhere, don't hesitate to leave *your* man.

1V1 DEFENDING

6

1v1 Defending Principles

R emember in the introduction when I said that *How We Defend* was a complement to what we did on the field? Well, here's a good example of what I'm
talking about. I can't adequately explain all the technical coaching points that
go into good 1v1 defending. That's material that we handled on the field. Our
handbook only covered the considerations a defender had to make when she was
engaged in a 1v1 battle. In other words, it covered the tactics of 1v1 defending,
starting with an attacker who has the ball and is dribbling at you.

From *How We Defend:*

1v1 Against an Opponent on the Dribble Who is Facing You:

- Whenever you are the first defender, you need to ask yourself,
  "What is the worst thing she can do to us?" Then take that thing
  away.

- She is only dangerous if she is in shooting range. Don't be afraid to retreat and

- consolidate with your teammates.

- It is HER job to initiate the fight. It is your job to delay it. It is her job to beat you. It is not your job to go and take the ball from her.

- Don't fight alone. Give your team a chance to help you.

- STALL. Wait for help if possible.

- The longer it takes, the more it favors the defending team.

- Don't cork the bottle. Give her another choice. Give her a chance to play slow.

- Don't tackle unless you're certain you'll win it or you have no choice. STAY PATIENT.

- Steer her into a less dangerous position and wait for help.

- If she plays sideways or backwards, you're doing a good job.

- Either the ball gets by or the man gets by. NEVER both.

- Realize when you are beaten and immediately do the next best thing – RECOVER CENTRALLY - REAL FAST. Get back behind the ball and find something to do.

Most of these are self-explanatory if you read the previous chapter. Again we are talking about getting behind the ball and hunting in a pack of two or more. Let's go into some detail about some of the material we haven't specifically covered.

Any experienced coach who reads this will immediately think of exceptions to the following examples (and the ones throughout this book), and they'd be exactly right. Defenders have to make decisions at warp speed. What might be the proper course of action in one moment might be completely wrong in the next. That's why you can't just hand this book to your players and expect them to have an answer for every situation they encounter. This book is intended to complement you, Coach, not replace you!

Whenever you are the first defender, you need to ask yourself, "What is the worst thing she can do to us?" Then take that thing away.
This might seem like common sense but believe me, it isn't. I'll give you an example:

Inside her own 18, a defender overplays a shot from a horrible angle and ends up conceding a square pass across the face of the goal.

Here's another one:

A center back lunges to block a difficult shot from 35 yards only to have the attacker cut the ball back and beat her on the dribble.

These things happen all the time. In the first example, the defender is better served by allowing a very low percentage shot and protecting against the slotted pass. In the second example, the defender is better off letting the attacker take a very low percentage shot than over-committing and being beaten on the dribble. Again, defenders have to understand what to take away and what to concede. Prioritizing is a critical part of being a smart defender.

The first defender – the one who confronts the ball – needs to be constantly calculating and recalculating the attacker's most dangerous option, and that option can and will change from one second to the next.

It is HER job to initiate the fight. It is your job to delay it. It is her job to beat you. It is not your job to go and take the ball from her.
The longer the first defender can draw out the battle, the more likely her team is to win it. Remember, smaller numbers favor the attacking team while bigger numbers favor the defending team. Fast play favors the attacking team because it limits the number of opponents who can get behind the ball. If the attacker wants to play slowly, don't talk her out of it! The more dancing she does on the ball, the more of your teammates can get back to help.

Don't cork the bottle. Give her another choice. Give her a chance to play slow.
I got the phrase 'Don't cork the bottle' from a book about the Civil War. One army had the chance to completely surround the other army, but chose to leave one road open. The logic was that with no alternative of escape, the surrounded army would fight with all it had to break through. By providing an illusion of escape, some soldiers would try to make a run for it, weakening their army. The point was that even offering a hope of escape would weaken the opponent's will to fight.

For our purposes, not corking the bottle means giving the player on the ball a chance to play slowly. For example, let's say the defender is in a 1v2 situation when the opposing forward receives the ball. If the forward acts quickly enough, she can play the killer pass to exploit that 2v1. How can we guarantee that she'll do so successfully? By flying in at her! With no opportunity to dribble, she'll play that killer pass and the attack will become more dangerous. However, if we lay off her a bit, maybe she'll take an extra touch or two, and that will give us the chance to organize defensively and neutralize the threat.

This is a high-level tactical moment that requires a high soccer IQ and some ultra-fast decision making on the defender's part.

Don't tackle unless you have no choice or you are invited to by a bad touch. STAY PATIENT.

Defenders are the most vulnerable when they attempt to tackle, because their bodies are committed in a direction that is typically away from their goal. They are even more committed if they go to ground.

Don't misconstrue this principle. If a defender can win the tackle, then by all means she should do just that. But when a player is running at you with the ball, typically, the player who commits first loses. Our objective is, as often as possible, to turn a 1v1 into a 1v2. We do that by staying patient and drawing out the battle so our teammates can get back to help us.

Steer her into a less dangerous position and wait for help.

A less dangerous position can mean a few different things, but typically it will come down to one of these few variables:

- A Wider Position – We want to funnel attacks away from our goal.
- Where You Have Help – Help can come in the form of a teammate or a boundary.
- Where She Doesn't Have Help – Sometimes we may have to funnel her to the inside if the most dangerous option is a pass to a player in a wider position.
- Her Weak Foot – When a player is in shooting range, particularly in the middle of the field, take away her window to shoot with her strong foot. The same could apply to a player who only goes one way with her dribble. If we know she wants to beat us to her right, we may have to force her onto her left, even if that puts her in a more central position.

If she plays sideways or backwards, you're doing a good job.

Remember, you can't take away everything. As the first defender, your primary job is to stop the ball from penetrating past you. You don't always need to come away with the ball to be a great defender. Take joy in the little victories. Sideways and backwards won't hurt you. If you've prevented the ball from penetrating, you've done something right!

Either the ball gets by or the man gets by. NEVER both.
I hate to say it, but when you are isolated in a 1v1, you can't let the opponent just breeze by you. When you tackle, you've got to hit something. If you don't, that opponent will be long gone.

Realize when you are beaten and immediately do the next best thing —
RECOVER CENTRALLY - REAL FAST. Get back behind the ball and find
something to do.
When a defender gets beat 1v1, that's a mistake and everyone makes them and coaches have to make peace with that. The real issue is what that defender does once she's been beaten. If she takes a half-second break for loathing and self-pity, she's made the second mistake, and that's the one we can't afford.

When you've been beaten, you've got to immediately — and I do mean *im-mediately* — move into damage control mode. So first things first, work your tail off to get between the ball and the goal. This is where a lot of outside backs lose the plot.

When beaten in the wide corridor of the field, a lot of outside backs will try to run the attacker down from behind and most of them never get there. If you can run her down, by all means, do it! But in the likely event that she is long gone, you've got to take a different route. Remember that the shortest distance between two points is a straight line. The first point is the ball and the second point is the near post of our goal. That's the most efficient angle of dribble for the attacker. Instead of chasing in the attacker's wake, choose a spot somewhere between the ball and the near post. The idea is to get to that spot as quickly as possible and hope to get there before the attacker so you get a second crack at her. Incidentally, it's not only when you've been beaten on the dribble that this recovery run makes sense. If you've been beaten by a pass, this also applies. By the same token, if the outside back has been beaten, the center back may have to make this same type of recovery run. The idea remains the same: Run to where she's going, not where she's at.

Recovery Run

In this diagram, the right back has been beaten on a pass to the left wing. The dotted line represents the most efficient angle of dribble for that attacker. The solid line represents a good recovery run for the defender that might give her a chance to confront the attacker.

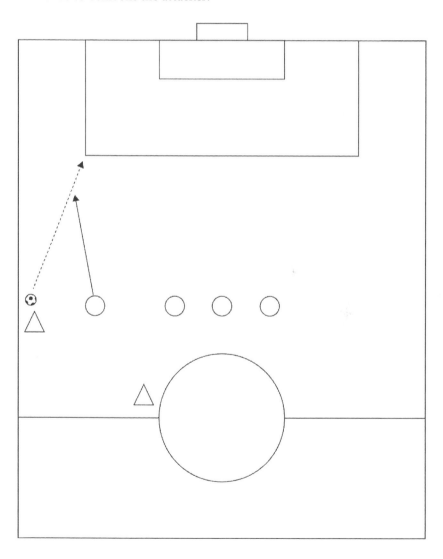

Recovery Run for Center Back

In this diagram, it is the center back who makes the recovery run to cover for the beaten outside back. Now the outside back's objective is to recover inside of the center back.

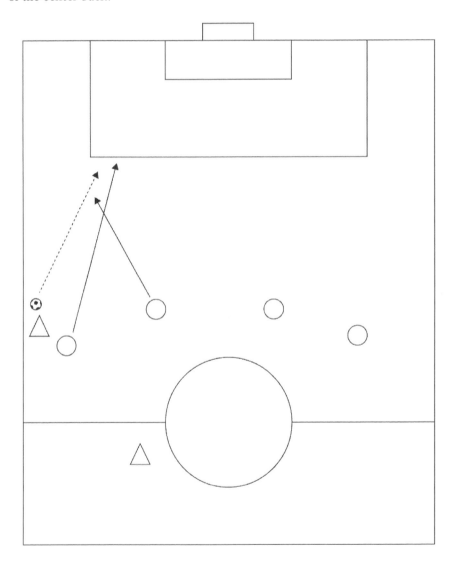

7

Individual Defending Questions

From *How We Defend:*

When you are the first defender, you must assess what you are willing to give away.

- A 1v1 dribble, or a pass sideways / backwards?
- A slow dribble angled away from goal, or a pass up the gut?
- A fast dribble angled away from goal, or a pass up the gut?
- A shot from a bad angle, or a good cross?
- A shot to the near post, or the attacker cutting back on the dribble?
- A narrow cross or a dangerous one?
- A throw-in or a cross?
- A cross or a corner kick?
- A long range (ambitious) shot or a dangerous pass?

We cannot take away everything. If you take away the middle you give away the outside. If you take away forward, you give away backward. Those are the easy ones.

A defender's brain can never stop working. You've constantly got to decide what you are willing to concede in order to protect against that which would do us the most harm. Defenders always need to be asking themselves questions during the run of play. These questions help prioritize the defender's immediate objective.

What is the worst thing that could happen right now?
When an opponent is about to take an unpressured shot from fourteen yards, it's pretty obvious what the worst thing that could happen will be. But a lot of times it's not so obvious. Sometimes conceding a shot is better than overplaying that shot and getting beat on the dribble or by a pass. Knowing the worst-case scenario is the key to prioritizing.

Is she dangerous? Can she shoot with a realistic chance to score?
Is the ball-carrier the biggest threat? If she's in a dangerous shooting position, then disrupting that shot might be the obvious choice.

Who is dangerous?
If the player on the ball isn't the most dangerous, then who is? Preventing a pass to that player might be the top priority.

Is she hurting me? Do I have to commit?
If she's not hurting you, you can afford to be more patient. If she's about to hurt you, then you may have to commit. The threat level dictates the defender's decision.

An attacker with her back to the goal isn't dangerous until she starts to turn. An attacker dribbling toward the sideline poses no threat to score. In these examples the defender can afford to be patient. That obviously isn't the case if the attacker is trying to dribble past the center back and into the 18.

What are our numbers?
When numbers are bad, delay, delay, delay! Give your team a chance to get back and help if at all possible. When numbers are good, you can afford to be more aggressive.

Can I delay her and wait for help?
If the answer is yes, then delay. If not, then get ready to put in your tackle.

Can I put her on her weak foot?
Some excellent players are completely one-footed. Putting a player on her weak foot can end a lot of potentially dangerous attacks.

If I was her, what would I do? (Example — We're running at a full sprint. Would I try to cross it or cut it back?)
The only advantage I enjoyed when I was converted to defender was that I had spent ten years as an attacker. That experience gave me the opportunity to evaluate the attacker's situation and helped me predict what his next move might be. I was always asking myself, *'What would I do if I was him?'* Defenders can't just be wrecking balls; they also have to be thinkers. Anticipating the attacker's next move can give you the half-step that wins the battle.

We're going to move into other individual defending scenarios in the next few chapters, but the concept never changes. Defenders have to prioritize their actions, and that begins with recognizing the biggest threat at any given moment. Remember, above all else, our decisions should be governed by whatever will make it most difficult for the opponent to score.

8

Individual Defending Technique

H ere are some of the key points for individual defending against an attacker who is facing you and advancing:

Make Him Predictable — Angle your approach to force him to the less dangerous side. If you have a covering defender, this will help him read the play and cheat.

Stance — Don't square your hips to the attacker. If you remember that it's the attacker's job to initiate the action, why make her job easier by being caught flat-footed? Give yourself the best possible body position to react to whatever the attacker does by keeping one foot in front of the other in a balanced stance. Think of it this way: If you and the attacker were about to get into a foot race, would you want to start that race with your back to the finish line?

Balance — This is the most common technical mistake defenders make. Because they've been coached to stay low, they translate that to mean 'Get your face as close as possible to the ball' and therefore their balance is all catty-wampus. This 1v1 duel will likely culminate in a foot race, and the finish line is behind you. Adjust your body weight as if you're about to run a race in that direction. Your body weight should be on your back leg and you should have a backward lean. Here's a simple way to evaluate your stance: Imagine a line starting from the knee cap of your front leg and extending straight into the sky. If your head or shoulder is touching or in front of that line, your body weight is too far forward.

Head Fake — It's not just attackers who can fake. As an attacker is dribbling at you, throw a quick lunge toward him as if you are committing yourself to engage. Make sure you have a solid four-yard cushion because your fake may bait the attacker into taking a long touch to get by you. If he does, you don't want to be so close to him that he can run right by you. In a perfect world, your lunge will induce the attacker to do just that — take a long touch that you'll be waiting to steal. More often though, a good head fake will break the attacker's dribbling rhythm for a moment and slow down the attack.

Tunnel Vision — When you're engaged in a 1v1 duel, focus your vision entirely on the attacker's feet and the ball. Try not to see anything above his knees. This will help prevent you from biting on upper body fakes. Don't worry about what his hips and shoulders are doing; the ball is the only thing that matters.

Patience — I can't possibly say this enough: It's the attacker's job to make something happen, not yours. The longer the duel lasts, the more it favors the defending team.

Commit — When you tackle, commit to it! Show some courage and try to pop the ball. In other words, no half-tackles!

1v1 Posture

A: The defender's head is out in front of her lead foot, so her body weight is too far forward.

B: The defender's stance is low but balanced to turn and run if the attacker pushes the ball past her.

A. 1v1 Bad Posture

B. 1v1 Balanced Stance

9

The World's Greatest Cue

A pply this when you're defending 1v1 out near the sideline and you'll look like a genius.

There's a time to be patient and a time to be more aggressive. Knowing the difference will determine the outcome of a lot of your 1v1 duels.

When you're defending 1v1 out on the flank and being patient and slowing down the ball-carrier, you need to look for moments to switch the balance of power to your favor. I'm going to give you a tiny but excellent cue to take charge of the confrontation.

Imagine a right winger is in the final 20 yards of the field with the ball at his feet. He takes a touch with the outside of his right foot. Although he is still facing the end-line, the ball is just wide of his right hip. That's the cue to make your move!

When the attacker puts the ball between his body and the sideline, *immediately* close down on him! By putting the ball on the outside of his body, he is giving you the chance to seal him off from the goal and all of his teammates. You've got to jump and jump fast! If you don't, he'll quickly move the ball back between himself and the goal. Even if you don't win the ball from him directly, you will dramatically slow down the attack and that's good for your team.

When the attacker gives you a gift like this, take him up on it! If he gives you the opportunity to pin him against the sideline, don't let him off the hook!

Later we'll see how recognizing this cue can also come in very handy when defending a 2v1.

10

1v1– Attacker Back to Pressure

We're going to be discussing a very specific scenario where you're on the back of an attacker who is checking back toward his own goal to receive a pass. Let me be clear: anytime you can be first to the ball, do it! I'm not trying to talk you out of it. If you can step in front and destroy the play or take the ball cleanly, go for it! This chapter is about those times when you won't get there before the attacker and he's going to receive the ball.

When the player you are marking is about to receive the ball while facing his own goal, the defender enjoys one distinct advantage: The attacker is facing the wrong way. As long as that's the case, he can't hurt you. That's why your first objective should be to keep him facing that direction. We don't want to let that player turn!

Here are some important points to back-to-pressure defending.

Get/Be/Stay Touch Tight

Let's say that the forward is checking back to receive a pass and you are tight on his back. You want to be close enough to pressure, but not so close that he can easily turn you. An arm's length is an ideal distance to be from the attacker when he receives the ball. We call this distance *touch tight*. If he tries to turn the ball in behind you with his first touch, that arm's length is your head start in the race to the ball. If you're too tight to the attacker, you give away your head start. Also, being too tight might make it impossible to see the ball, a point we'll cover in a moment. If, on the other hand, you're further than an arm's length, the attacker will have room to turn and face you, and you've just given away the one advantage you enjoyed.

Many times an attacker will try to break free of your pressure by taking the ball back toward his own goal. If the attacker retreats with the ball, don't let him gain separation. Keep him within that arm's length.

Prepare Your Body to Run the Other Direction

Again the forward is checking back to receive a pass and you are tight on his back. Keep in mind that the direction he wants to go is not the direction the both of you are currently traveling. As he is about to receive the ball, there's an excellent chance he's trying to figure out how to get the ball in behind you. If he wants to turn it into a footrace, you have to remember that the finish line is behind you, so prepare your body to run a race in that direction. When the attacker takes his first touch, you shouldn't be leaning forward, but rather leaning slightly backward and your weight should be on your back leg and not your front one.

See the Ball

Too many defenders believe that being tight to the attacker means having your nose on his neck. When the ball is arriving, you want to see it in the whole way. This is where that arm's length and preparing your body will come in handy. Even as you are running with that checking attacker, you should try to stay low. Try to peak around his hip to make sure you keep the ball in sight.

Why? Because how in the world will you know what to do if you can't see the ball!

Another excellent reason for staying low and seeing the ball is that it prevents you from looking at the attacker's shoulders, and a lot of attackers are excellent with shoulder fakes. If you spend a lot of time watching an attacker's shoulders and hips, you're going to spend a lot of time getting dusted! The attacker's upper body will tell you nothing but lies and damned lies. Don't take the bait! If you stay low and focus your eyes on the ball, you won't have to worry about this problem.

Leave a Foot in the Path of the Ball

As the ball is arriving and it becomes obvious that the attacker is going to try and run by you, leave one foot in the path of the ball until the last possible second in case he tries to dummy. Seeing the ball will let you know exactly where to leave that foot.

Be a Gnat

If the attacker decides to hold the ball instead of turning with it, try to unsettle him by staying touch tight and being as aggressive as possible. Hound him! There should be a lot of physical contact. You should be as annoying as the gnat that just won't stop buzzing around your head. The idea is to do all this while not drawing a foul.

Use Your Front Leg to Corral the Attacker to One Side

If the attacker holds the ball, extend your leg so your front foot forms a fence that will deter/prevent the attacker from turning toward that side. While your front leg fences in one side of the attacker, your head should be looking around the opposite hip to see the ball.

Don't Ever Give Away Goal-Side

Sometimes that attacker will hold the ball under his foot and invite you to take a stab at it. Don't take the bait! He wants you to lunge at the ball and when you do – *POOF!* – he's gone! Remember, it's his job to make something happen, not yours. Don't ever give away goal-side! Don't be afraid to wait. Don't go lunging for the ball just because you got bored. He can't hurt you if he's facing his own goal. Think big picture: The longer this battle takes, the more of your team-mates will get behind the ball.

Obstruct and Retreat

Often times an attacker who is holding the ball will play a square or negative pass to a teammate and then try to roll off you to receive a return pass in behind you. Don't let him go freely. Get your body into his path and keep him in your back pocket as you retreat into that dangerous space.

1v1 Stance - Attacker Back-to-Pressure

A: As the attacker receives the ball, the defender is too upright and too tight, so she is unbalanced and in no position to see the ball.

B: The defender is touch-tight as the ball arrives at the attacker's feet. She stays low and peeks around the attacker's hip to see the ball. Her bodyweight is prepared to run back toward her own goal.

A. 1v1 Back to Pressure Bad

B. 1v1 Back to Pressure Good

1v1 Stance - Attacker Holding the Ball
Back-to-Pressure - Good

As the attacker holds the ball, the defender uses her forward leg to corral the attacker to one side. She stays low and peeks around the attacker's opposite hip to see the ball. The defender's bodyweight is prepared to run back toward her own goal.

11

1v1 – Attacker Facing the Sideline

This is one of those mistakes that happens pretty regularly and there's absolutely no excuse for it if you remember your principles.

An attacker is chasing a ball toward the sideline and you're chasing him. His body language tells you that he's either going to dribble negatively or play a negative pass. You take the bait and try to take away his negative option. Much to your surprise, he does a step-over and the next thing you know, he's gotten goal-side of you and is dribbling down the line.

This is one of those times when the defender forgets that protecting the goal is more important than getting the ball back. If you remember that protecting the goal is more important, then you won't be been fazed by the step-over because your sole objective will be to get yourself between the ball and the goal and to defend from a goal-side position.

Remember your priorities. Get your body between the ball and the goal. That's the only way to protect your goal. Don't worry about what he might do; just do what you're supposed to do. You've got to be willing to concede the negative dribble/pass in order to take away goal-side. He can't hurt you if he's going backwards. Never sacrifice a backward movement for a forward one.

12

1v1 – Attacker is Facing You But Not Advancing

Let's say an attacker who is facing you has just received the ball and killed it close to her body. You are the defender who will pressure the ball. Let's say your starting position is ten yards away from the attacker when she receives the ball.

As defenders, we don't want that attacker playing a penetrating pass and we don't want her to build up the courage and momentum to run at us. She is at a standstill, and we want to keep her that way. Keeping in mind our priorities, here are some key points for pressuring that attacker.

Close Ground Fast – With ten yards between you, the attacker has a lot of options to play forward, not the least of which is the opportunity to play over the top of you. The farther you are from her, the more opportunities she has to play a vertical pass. With each step you take toward her, the vertical options begin to dissipate. You want to turn those ten yards into five yards as quickly as possible, if for no other reason than to prevent her from playing over your head. In other words, we want a quick start.

Quick Start, Slow Arrival – If you just go sprinting at the attacker, she's going to sidestep you like a matador does to a charging bull, so we've got to slow down in a hurry. You cover the first five or six yards at a full sprint and then immediately put on the brakes and cover the last few yards with short, quick, choppy steps. Once you've taken away her vertical options, now it's truly a 1v1 and your focus has to turn to the player on the ball. Evaluate her with each step you take so you'll know what adjustments you need to make in your angle of approach and your level of aggression.

Get Her Head Down – When her eyes go down to the ball, the advantage swings to you because she's no longer focusing on her teammates. Now you don't have to worry as much about her passing the ball; now she's got to figure a way out of this on her own. This is a tremendous visual cue and you have to recognize it. When you get her head down, quickly close ground with small, choppy steps. Once her head goes down, we don't want it coming back up.

Go After the Ball – If she lets you get close enough, challenge for the ball. Don't just stand there and shadow her, otherwise she'll get her head up and her teammates will return as options. When you get close to her, step up your aggression!

If the attacker starts advancing at you, then you've got to revert back to your sound 1v1 defending techniques and this may require a bit of shuffle-retreating.

13

1v1 Shot-Blocking

I had been coaching for more than a decade before I started teaching shot-blocking. The inspiration came from the 2003 Stanley Cup Playoffs when my Philadelphia Flyers were playing the Tampa Bay Lightning. It was a frustrating series for the Flyers, mainly because of Tampa Bay's exceptional shot-blocking prowess. It seemed like none of the Flyers' shots were making it to the net. And I never forgot it.

Adding shot-blocking to the agenda has had a huge impact on teams I've coached. It's amazing how hard it is to score when your shots don't reach the goal.

Shot-blocking, first and foremost, requires courage, and this book won't give you that. To be an effective shot-blocker, you've got to want to get hit by the ball. It's that simple. Now, if you can muster up the nerve to stand in front of a missile for the good of the cause, I can give you some tips to make you more effective.

Angle of Approach – Let's look at the diagram on the next page. The attacker has the ball at the top of the 18 and is prepped to shoot. There is a window from the ball to the goal. The defender's objective is to get in that window and clog it. This often means running laterally instead of stepping out toward the shooter, as indicated by the solid arrow. Incidentally, one way that players try to disguise their lack of courage is by stepping out toward the shooter – as indicated by the dotted arrow – saving them from getting into the path of the ball. If you actually want to block the shot, you've got to put your body in front of the ball. The solid arrow is the proper path.

Shot-Blocking Approach

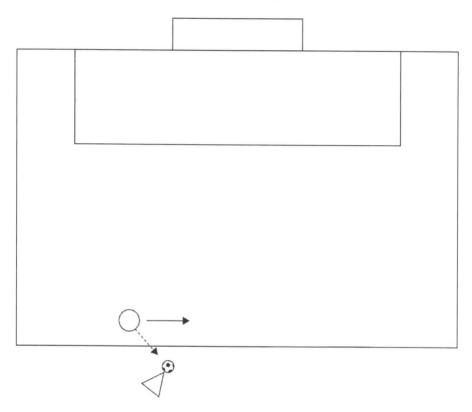

Half-Step – Once we've clogged the shooting window, the attacker may try dribbling laterally to create a new window. If she invites a tackle, then by all means, tackle! But be careful about over-committing when you are in shooting range because if you gamble and lose, the attacker may end up with a great chance to score. If tackling is too risky, stay patient and mirror her movements as she heads laterally. Try to keep your lead foot a half-step ahead of the ball to keep the shooting window clogged.

Hands Down – When preparing to shot- or cross- block, defenders must learn to keep their hands down and preferably behind their backs. Failure to do so will often end up in creating a handball, and since most shot-blocking takes place close to the goal... well, you see where I'm going with that. It takes a tremendous amount of courage to put your hands behind your back and square up to a shooter, but great defenders must have courage.

The Chuck Berry – Let's say you are 1v1 against an attacker on top of the 18. She's moving laterally, hesitating and accelerating, trying to create a window for her shot. As long as you keep your lead foot in front of the ball, that window won't appear. But if you lunge too hard to one direction, she'll cut the ball back across you and fire with her other foot. That's why it's important to take small, choppy steps and to not let your legs cross. My favorite video of this technique doesn't come from a soccer player, but from a rock-n-roll legend – Chuck Berry.

Check out Mr. Berry playing *Nadine* at www.youtube.com/ watch?v=Cm8ktxzaumg. At the 1:18 mark of the clip, Chuck is giving a textbook example of shot-blocking technique. The idea is to keep your lead foot off the ground as much as possible to prevent the ball from flying over it. You can only do this if you're taking small, choppy steps like the rock-n-roll Hall of Famer.

The Chuck Berry

The defender demonstrates the Chuck Berry shot-blocking technique.

A. Chuck Berry Front

B. Chuck Berry Rear

14

Shot-Blocking
While Running
Toward the Corner

Let's say that the attacker and defender are inside the 18, running practically side by side at an angle away from the goal. The attacker has a half-step on the defender and the defender is in full stride, so the Chuck Berry won't do any good.

In this situation, the defender's job is to take away the back half of the goal as a shooting option. Take away the window to the far post and give the goalkeeper responsibility for protecting the front half of the goal. If the shot goes low to the back post, there's an excellent chance it's going to end up in the net. On the other hand, the goalkeeper stands an excellent chance to make a save if the shot comes to the front half of the goal.

Also, there comes a time when a shot is actually the best thing you can concede. As you are running wider and wider, you've got to evaluate the angle that the attacker has left to shoot and whether or not a shot would even be dangerous. In this situation, if a shot wouldn't be reasonably dangerous, then I assure you that you're better off playing against a cut-back on the dribble or a square pass.

Too often a defender in this situation will over-commit and slide to shot-block. Believe me, this is exactly what the attacker is hoping you'll do because he knows how unlikely he is to score while sprinting away from the goal at top speed. When you sell out to shot-block, he'll cut the ball back while you go flying by, then a whole new world of better options will appear for him.

When you get to this point, put some faith in your goalkeeper and tap your brakes to prepare for the cut-back. Invite the attacker to take a difficult shot and just worry about preventing the new worst thing that could happen.

15

Cross-Blocking

Before we get into cross-blocking technique, let me give you some excellent advice. If a crossing situation is developing, whenever possible, get yourself outside of the 18 before engaging the attacker. I've seen many occasions of a defender setting up to cross-block a step inside of the 18 when she could've just as easily set up a step wide of it. It's not uncommon for a cross to deflect off a defender's arm and result in a hand ball. If you fall victim to that type of bad luck, you're obviously better off conceding a free kick wide of the 18 than a penalty kick. As we discussed in shot-blocking, you also want to try to keep your hands and arms down by your side or behind your back if at all possible when attempting to block a cross.

Cross-blocking technique is very similar to shot-blocking. The idea is still to keep your foot up in front of the ball as much as possible. Ultimately we want to take away the window to a dangerous cross.

The most common mistake a defender makes here is to over-commit. This happens when the defender realizes she'll be a half-second too late to block the cross. She'll lunge, leave her feet and turn her back to the ball. This leaves her exceptionally prone to a cut-back from the attacker. If you're flying through the air or facing the wrong direction when the attacker cuts back, you're toast. You've got to have the courage to square up to the attacker even when she's about to rifle in a cross.

The most important part of cross-blocking is your positioning before the cross is hit. If at all possible, stay a half-step ahead of the ball and start working your Chuck Berry. Let me tell you why this half-step is so important. If you're a half-step ahead of the ball and waving your lead foot in the air, there's an excellent chance you're going to block any dangerous cross. A lot of cross-blocks turn into corner kicks, and we don't want to hand out corner kicks any more than absolutely necessary. The half-step approach tends to angle a good percentage of the blocked crosses back toward the sideline instead of the end-line.

There's also an excellent chance that if the ball gets past your foot, it's because the cross has been poorly delivered and is going to either angle out of bounds, wide of the near post, or within the keeper's domain at the near post. The half-step method takes away the most dangerous window for delivery of the ball and results in a lot of crosses that come in too narrow to be effective.

Also, there are times when you don't want to get in the way of a cross, and you need a high soccer IQ to recognize these moments. If the crosser's dribble has her angling out toward the corner flag or she is totally off balance, there's an excellent chance her cross will end up sailing over the end-line and your team will be awarded a goal kick. The last thing you want is to have that lame cross deflect off of you, turning *your* goal kick into *their* corner kick. If you are convinced that the cross has no chance of reaching the target area, just get out of the way.

Finally, there are times when you and the attacker are flying down the sideline at full speed and you absolutely know you won't get there in time to block her cross, even if you slide. In these moments, when the attacker cocks her leg to begin her crossing motion, you may be able to bait her into a cut back by faking like you're going to lunge. Take a big step and straighten up like you're going airborn, then slam on the brakes. Maybe you'll get lucky and she'll take the bait and you'll get another crack at her.

The free PDF at www.soccerpoet.com contains my two favorite shot-blocking and cross-blocking drills.

2V1 DEFENDING

16

Defending a 2v1

The 2v1 is often the most threatening situation a defender will face. These situations require patience, cunning and decisiveness. You're outnumbered, so you're going to stall and hope for help, but when you recognize it's time to go, you've got to commit to your choice and go in with everything you've got.

The first key, and one that too many defenders never realize, is to do your math. If you want to make good decisions, you have to actually recognize that you're outnumbered. That should be the first thing you calculate. Once you recognize you're outnumbered, the following menu of options should pop into your head.

Delay – When you are the defender in a 2v1, make no mistake about it, you are on the defensive. Remember, it's not your job to make something happen; that job falls to the attackers. Your job is to give your team the best chance to prevent a goal, and you do that by drawing out the battle for as long as you can. Delaying, mainly by retreating and staying between the ball and the goal, gives your teammates the best chance of getting back to help you.

There are scenarios when your help just won't get to you in time. It doesn't matter, keep stalling. Every second you delay the attack gives your team a better chance at thwarting the attack. Think of it this way: Maybe the attackers get off a dangerous shot, but it hits the post and deflects back into the 18. The longer it took them to take that shot, the better chance your teammates have of getting to that rebound. Every second matters.

Pick Your Moment — Sometimes the attacking pair will give you a chance to turn that 2v1 into a 1v1. This is a landmark moment if you're ready for it. You've got to be on the lookout for cues that give you the chance to better your odds. Maybe the first attacker will take a touch to the wide-side of his body, or take a touch that's a little longer than it should be, and that will give you a chance to seal off his teammate and turn the situation into a 1v1. When one of these moments occurs, you've got to pounce! If they invite you to turn a 2v1 into a 1v1, *GO!* Don't give them the chance to correct their mistake.

Damage Control — In these situations, you won't always be able to prevent a shot, but if there's going to be a shot, you want to do whatever you can to affect its chances of scoring. Anything you can do to physically unbalance the attacker or steer her to a slightly worse angle hurts her chances of putting the ball in the net.

17

2v1 Up the Gut

A clear cut 2v1 coming straight at your center back is bad, bad news. If a center back finds herself in this situation, she'll need to apply a healthy dose of savvy to survive it. When the attack is coming up the middle, there are two mistakes that the center back commonly makes.

The first mistake is losing patience and committing to the ball too early and too high up the field. It's important not to over-commit to the ball, particularly when there is space in behind you. If you commit to the ball, the attacker's job is very easy. She'll simply pass the ball to her teammate and you'll be cleanly beaten.

The other common mistake is that the defender will try to evenly split the width between the two attackers. It makes sense in theory, but in practice it typically ends up with an attacker scoring a goal.

This is one of those situations where you've got to look for your chance to turn the 2v1 into a 1v1, and all things being equal, you want the ball-carrier to be the one that you duel with. So as you retreat, instead of splitting the distance between the two players, shade to the side of the higher attacker. Instead of a 50-50 split, slide about 2/3 of the distance toward the higher attacker. We want the ball-carrier to keep dribbling.

Okay, this is where this gets a little complicated. Everyone prefers to dribble in a rhythm. So a two-step rhythm would go: touch, step, step, touch, step, step, touch. We're going to be super intelligent defenders and look for a gap in that rhythm.

There is a gap in time between the touches of a ball-carrier. The biggest gap between touches begins immediately as the ball is leaving her foot. At that moment, the ball is running away from her and she has to catch up to it. Each step she takes gets her closer to taking her next touch. So we are looking for the moment when the ball is just coming off of her foot, because that's the biggest window of time that we'll have to manipulate the situation. That is *our moment*.

When you pick your moment, that's when you abandon the higher attacker and make your move to seal off the ball-carrier. You've got to angle your run in such a way that it cuts off a pass to the second attacker. We don't want to concede a square pass or any pass that is angled forward that puts that second attacker back into the equation.

If you choose this method, try to make your move about 30 yards out from goal. Otherwise, you might not get there in time to disrupt the shot.

If you do this properly and the heavens smile down and it goes as planned, you'll now find yourself 1v1 with the first attacker. You won't be between her and the goal, but you'll be side-by-side running toward the end-line. At this point you may be able to get in a tackle or at least disrupt the shot.

Defending a 2v1 Up the Gut 1

The defender immediately retreats and shades toward the higher attacker to deter a pass.

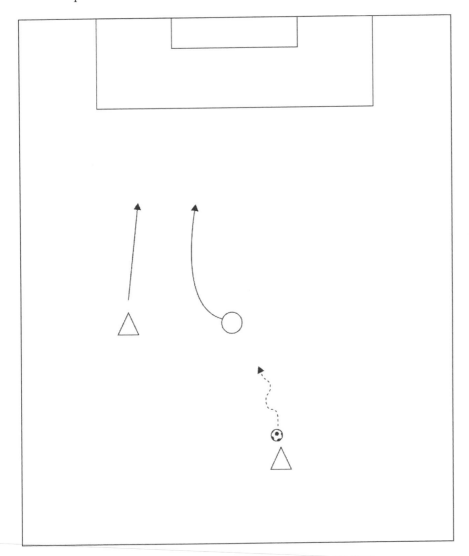

When to Over-Commit to the Ball

In the same situation of a 2v1 coming up the gut, you may occasionally encounter an attacker who makes your life easy. In advance of the ball, the smart attacker won't run straight ahead; she'll curl her run away from you. This creates the separation for a passing seam while also helping her to stay onside. However, if she hasn't quite figured this out yet, she'll sprint straight ahead, staying level with you as you retreat. If you notice her doing this, she is begging to be called offside.

Once again, time the dribbler's rhythm and pick your moment. When you make your move, jump straight out in front of the ball-carrier and commit solely to defending the dribble. Make sure you leave a passing lane open to her offside teammate. Invite the pass to the offside teammate! Beg for it! More than anything else, we want the ball-carrier to play that forward pass!

Make no mistake about it, this is a big gamble. If you do this, you are committing to putting in a tackle if the ball-carrier doesn't pass. When you jump out at the ball-carrier, failure is not an option, so you've got make darn sure that the attacker doesn't dribble cleanly by you.

18

2v1 On the Flank

This is a situation that outside backs commonly encounter. Typically the higher attacker is out on the sideline while the ball-carrier is coming from a deeper and more central position.

This isn't as immediately threatening as the 2v1 coming up the gut. As a matter of fact, in this situation, there are typically other defenders/attackers to the inside of the ball. In the last chapter, the 2v1 was the whole picture. This 2v1 is a microcosm of the big picture, but it's a 2v1 nonetheless. This is why I said earlier that the first step for the defender is actually recognizing she's in a 2v1.

Here's my very simple advice for positioning yourself in this situation: Stay inside of the ball and one step ahead (goal-side) of the higher attacker.

Remember, we want to force play wide. That's why we stay inside of the ball. We want to protect the middle against the attacker's dribble toward the goal and invite the pass out to the sideline.

We stay one step ahead of the higher attacker so she can't beat us with her first touch when she receives a pass.

Again we delay, delay, delay and hope that our center back has time to shift over and help.

The next diagram shows the proper positioning of the defender in this 2v1.

2v1 On the Flank

The defender stays inside of the ball and one step ahead of the higher attacker as indicated by the dashed lines.

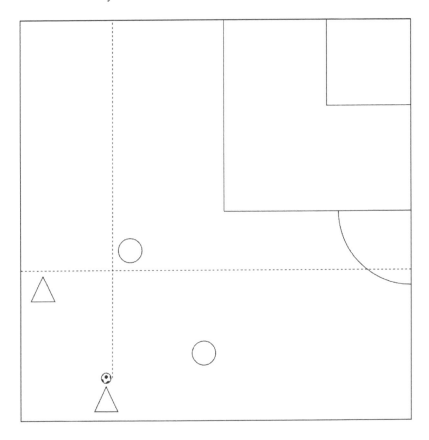

19

The Great Mistake

E ven though this chapter deals with the exact same situation we just discussed, its importance warrants a chapter of its own. I believe that this chapter alone is worth the price of the book, so pay attention. If you take nothing else from this book, please take this!

Let me begin with a very simple premise: *Never run into the front end of a 2v1.*

Let's look at the same scenario that was facing our outside back in the previous diagram. What will happen if the outside back steps up to confront the ball? Obviously the ball-carrier will simply pass the ball to her teammate on the sideline. That pass will eliminate the outside back, putting her team in danger. To cover for her mistake, the center back will have to slide out to confront the ball, and our defensive shape is now further compromised.

Why is this chapter so important? Because defenders do this all the time! This is the single-most common positional mistake that defenders make. It's indicative of a defending mindset that prioritizes getting the ball back ahead of protecting the goal.

I could never quite get my head around this one. I don't know why the outside back would choose to jump up to the ball. It's positional suicide! It just doesn't make any sense, but it happens over and over and over again at all levels. I see it all the time at the college level and even saw it happen twice in a women's U-20 World Cup match. It's an epidemic of silliness! And if national teams are doing it, then chances are your team is also.

Nothing good happens when the outside back jumps into the front end of a 2v1, so don't! Stay patient, remember what's important and protect the goal.

20

A Time to Surrender

S ometimes it's worth a gamble for an outside back to abandon her mark and step to an opposing player who is about to receive the ball. If she gets there in time, she can either win the ball cleanly or destroy the play with a tackle. But if she gets there late, she'll find herself in the front end of a 2v1... and that's bad.

If you decide to make that gamble and after a few steps you realize you won't get there in time, don't turn one mistake into a bigger one. You have to know when to surrender. Cut your losses and retreat as fast as you can. Put yourself in position to keep the play in front of you and force the ball wide. Remember that your top priority is to keep the ball out of your net.

21

2v1 Layoffs – The Gamble

L et's say you are on a forward's tail as she checks back to the ball near midfield, facing her own goal. She has a teammate in support, seven yards behind her. You know that she's going to lay the ball back to her teammate. What do you do?

Well, that depends. There's allegedly an exception to every rule, and here is the exception to our *'Never run into the front of a 2v1'* rule.

The safe play is to allow the ball back and deal with the player you're currently engaged with. But sometimes we can do better than that. We may be able to destroy the whole play, but it takes split-second decision-making and decisive action. If you read it right, you may be able to pop off your mark and vaporize the player receiving the layoff. But that's a gamble because you'll be running into the front end of a 2v1.

If you think you can get there in time, go and go fast! Angle your approach to eliminate a simple return pass and go in with everything you have to destroy that play, because if you fail, you're toast. Don't take this gamble unless you are almost 100% certain that you'll get there in time to destroy the play. If there is the slightest bit of doubt, just lay off.

I would only suggest this if the supporting player is within seven yards of the player who is playing her the ball. More than that is too much distance to cover safely, unless you know the lay-off is of poor quality, particularly if it's under-hit.

This is a decision that can come up quite often with throw-ins, where the player receiving the ball lays it back to the thrower.

22

Something Fishy – 2v1 Off the Ball

There will be times when you are in a 2v1 off the ball, marking the higher of the two players. That player will be checking back to the ball while the lower player will be streaking past you. This is a pretty common occurrence and if you don't play it properly, the opponent will be in behind you and your team will be in trouble!

There comes a time to release the player going back to his own goal so you can deal with the player who has become more dangerous – the one flying by you.

Some teams specialize in this movement. The winger will check back and toward the middle of the field with the sole hope of dragging you with him. At that moment, he doesn't even want the ball; he's just a decoy. He's trying to pull you back to the ball so the ball-carrier can play past the both of you to the attacker who is running toward your goal.

This isn't limited to wing play. Often times a center forward will check back as a center midfielder runs by him. It's the same dog with different fleas.

Being a smart defender means sniffing this out, and again that starts with recognizing that you're in a 2v1. The instant you recognize that something smells fishy, release the player you are marking and adjust to deal with the more dangerous player. Yes, you will be conceding the ball underneath, but that's the lesser of two evils. The player running toward your goal is the more dangerous opponent and that's the one who needs your attention.

Sometimes this type of movement isn't premeditated. Sometimes it just materializes because of the fortuitous movement of the opponent. Doesn't matter. Either way it's a big-time problem if you don't play it properly.

Something Fishy

This diagram illustrates a winger trying to drag the right back toward the ball so that his teammate can receive a ball in behind the defense. The outside back recognizes this, puts on the brakes and retreats to deal with the more imminent threat.

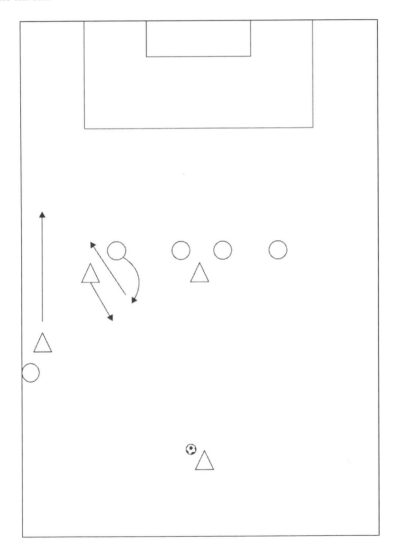

23

Committed in a 2v1 or 3v1

Continuing with the same situation as the previous chapter, there will be times when you commit to the player checking back to the ball as his teammate is advancing into the space you vacated. If the attacker you've latched onto receives the ball and then gets it to his advancing teammate, your team is in serious danger.

At this point, you are compromised and you have to realize it. Your number one priority has to be preventing the player on the ball from getting it to that advancing attacker. This means you can't let the attacker turn and you have to overplay to one side. If the advancing teammate is coming down your left side, you need to take away the left side and force the ball to go somewhere else. Whatever happens, do not let that first attacker get the ball to his advancing teammate!

The second problem you might run into is a ball back for a ball forward. A short layoff can put that advancing attacker back in play. Let's say the left wing has checked back toward the middle of the field to receive the ball with you on his back, while the opponent's left back is overlapping into the space you just vacated. You've cut off the winger from playing the ball directly, but a midfielder is supporting underneath him. If he lays that ball back to the midfielder, the midfielder will play that killer ball into the overlapping left back. This is a situation where you may want to take a foul to kill the play, as you are horribly compromised and the referee's whistle might be the only thing that saves you. But let's just continue on with the idea of not fouling. So what do you do?

Well, if the layoff is more than ten yards, you're better off bailing out and retreating. But if the layoff is shorter than ten yards, you'll need to get your courage on.

If at all possible, anticipate the layoff and explode after it, doing anything you can to get in the way of the next pass. Make sure the angle of your approach cuts out a ball to the overlapping left back. When you chase that layoff, you are taking a big but necessary gamble. Make sure it pays off by going in hard and fast and with reckless disregard for personal safety. At this point you've got to have the mindset of a Secret Service agent jumping in to take a bullet for the President. You've got be a hero! You've got to want that ball to hit you!

Committed in a 2v1

The overlapping left back has caught the opposing right back in a 2v1. The right back overplays against the unprotected side, preventing the attacker on the ball from turning that way.

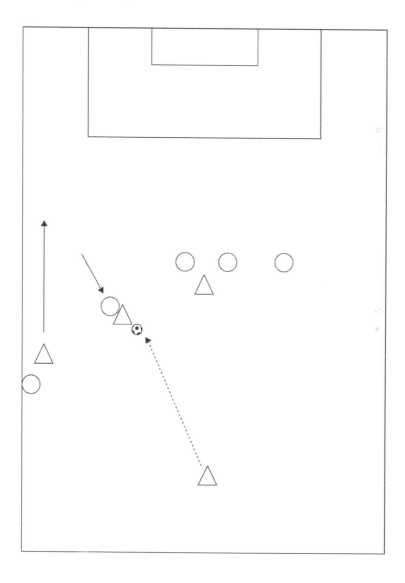

24

2v1 Marking on a Cross

When you're outnumbered in front of goal in a crossing situation, you have your hands full. If you latch on to the near post runner, you leave the back post runner free and that's no good. If you latch on to the back post runner, you leave the near post runner free and that's no good either. If you split the two, you accomplish absolutely nothing and that's even worse. So what do you do?

The near post runner is the more imminent threat because it involves a shorter cross and that means less time for you to make a play. It's also the easier of the two serves to execute and to finish. My suggestion is to loosely mark the near post runner and pay close attention to the serve. The idea is to discourage a near post cross, bait a far post cross and hope to make up ground while the ball is in flight.

Instead of being shoulder to shoulder with the near post runner, trail him by a step. If the serve comes into him, tighten up to destroy the play.

As soon as you recognize that the serve is going to the back post, release the near post runner, then turn and run to challenge at the back post. Also, if you recognize that the near post runner is arriving too early and will be well beyond the near post before the ball arrives, that's a cue to release him and start moving toward the back post runner. The gamble is that the near post runner now has a difficult finish since he has run himself beyond the frame of the goal.

Believe me, this is much easier said than done. Keep in mind we're talking about split-second decisions here. You are evaluating a lot of variables and they are moving at breakneck speed. Plus, you have to read the serve the instant it's off the server's foot. But since you're outnumbered, you've got to take some educated gambles.

Let me give you a bonus tip... Try to watch the server's eyes. I can't adequately express how important this is. More often than not, the last place the server looks (before looking back down at the ball) is the place where he intends to deliver the ball. Reading his eyes can give you a half-second head start to the target attacker.

1V2 DEFENDING PRESSURE – COVER

25

What is Pressure-Cover?

P ressure-cover is a defensive set-up where two defenders are tasked with stopping the forward progress of the ball. The first defender – the one who pressures the ball – is your pressure. The role of cover falls to the second defender. She is the first defender's wing-man.

The role of the pressuring defender is pretty simple: Don't get beat on the dribble and try to make the ball-carrier predictable.

The covering defender's multi-tasking is a bit more complex. While the first defender is focusing on a single opponent, the second defender is trying to manage a bigger picture with more moving parts.

The covering defender has two jobs:

1. Stop the ball if the first defender gets beat on the dribble.
2. Prevent a penetrating pass that would split the first and second defenders.

The second defender's job is critical. It is also critical that she understands the governing principles of our defensive system. If she doesn't, she's going to make a lot of positional mistakes.

In the next diagram we have a 2v2 situation with the attackers attacking toward the top of the page.

In Diagram A, the second defender has moved out from a goal-side position to mark an opponent who is behind the ball. This is bad because it leaves the first defender without cover. This is a vital distinction that defenders have to make. It might seem sensible to move forward to match up with the unmarked player, so players commonly make this mistake. But when the second defender moves forward, the numbers turn from 2v2 to 1v1, and 1v1 is a better equation for the attackers. If the attacker wins that 1v1 duel, there's no one to stop the ball. The second defender needs to be willing to concede the square/negative pass in order to cover the first defender. In short, the covering defender needs to stay goal-side of the first defender.

In Diagram B, the second defender is flat to the first defender. Again, this provides very little protection if the first defender is beaten on the dribble and does not protect against a pass that splits the two defenders.

In Diagram C, the second defender takes up a proper covering position. She concedes a negative pass to protect against a penetrating one. Also, she can come to the rescue if the first defender is beaten on the dribble.

There are many nuances to being a good covering defender, but they all begin with the simple premise that having two defenders behind the ball is better than having one. That means conceding sideways and backwards in order to protect against forward.

Covering Position – Bad, Bad, Good

A

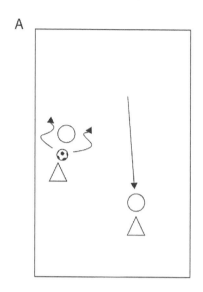

B

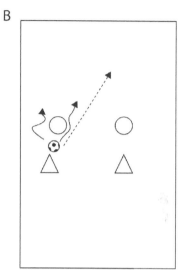

C

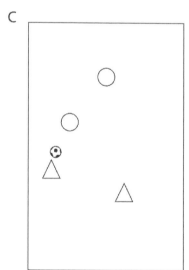

26

Coffin Corner – Pressure-Cover

During a training session at Ole Miss in October of 2009, our most talented striker, who I'll call Amie, was lamenting a drill where we were going to run our attackers against our defense. This was a pretty common drill for us and Amie was saying how it didn't serve the attackers because the attackers never had to play against a defense that set up like ours. She referred to our defenders as the *"Damn cover queens."* It was a tremendous compliment.

Pressure-Cover was *the* signature of our defense. In its simplest form, the idea was to funnel the ball into a corner where an opponent would be matched up 1v1 with our outside back. The outside back would force the attacker wide and down the line. As the attacker tried to run by the outside back, our center back would come across and annihilate her. Pressure and Cover.

I will say that this is a pretty old school set-up, but that didn't make it any less effective. The key is that each player understands her role and trusts her teammates to do their jobs, and that their timing is perfect.

The next diagram provides a typical situation that we would encounter at least a half-dozen times per game. The winger has the ball and is isolated against our right back. The right back's primary job is to cut off the middle. If the winger gets to the middle, she should have to go backwards to do so, even if just by a step or two. Once she has cut off the middle, the right back's job is to dare the winger to try to dribble by her on the outside. If the right back has a great chance to tackle, then by all means she should! But that's not her priority. Her priority is to make the attacker predictable for the center back by forcing the winger down the line. The outside back is setting the table for the center back.

The center back's job is initially to clog a central passing seam while simultaneously covering for the outside back in case she is beaten on the dribble. As the center back is doing that, she's also reading the situation and creeping closer to the fray. The more she's convinced that the attacker can't get to the middle, the more she can cheat toward the sideline.

The center back is waiting for one cue – a big, vertical touch from the winger – the touch that turns this duel into a footrace. The moment the winger takes that vertical touch, the center back must come flying across to destroy the play. As you see in the final diagram, at the moment of impact, the center back ends up wide of the outside back who immediately tucks in centrally once the center back commits to the challenge.

This is a lot easier on paper than in practice. It takes a lot of repetitions to get it right. And it takes a lot of trust. The outside back is basically setting herself up to get beat in the footrace, so she has to trust that the center back will appear at the right moment. The center back needs to cheat toward the sideline, so she needs to trust that the outside back won't let the attacker get to the middle. The timing has to be perfect. And finally, the center back has to sell out! When she goes, she has to commit to it 100%! You can get all the other pieces just right, but if the center back hesitates, you're going to have problems.

The ultimate victory in a coffin corner scenario is to emerge with the ball. We don't want our center back simply coming across and whacking the ball over the sideline if she has the chance to steal possession. And it won't always be the center back who ends up with the ball. These double-teams will often result in the outside back emerging with the ball. Either way, there will be opportunities for the defender without the ball to set a pick on the attacker that will help our team escape with the ball.

It's worth mentioning that the center back won't always have the freedom to provide cover. If the opponent has a numerical advantage in front of goal, the center back will have to stay inside to pick up a runner. Either way, it's important that the center back communicates to the outside back, and we'll discuss that further in just a bit.

One other word of caution... If you play like this, you absolutely cannot let the ball come out of that corner! You have two defenders committed far away from the goal they're supposed to be protecting, so as the saying goes, failure is not an option. You can't allow a cross and you can't allow the attacker to dribble through you. It just can't happen.

Coffin Corner

The outside back funnels the attacker to the corner as the center back slides over to make the tackle.

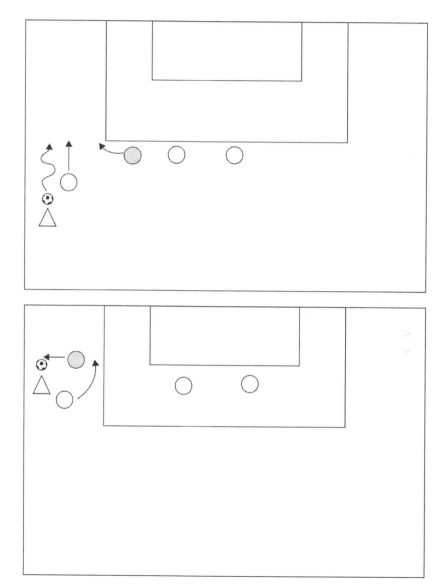

27

Communicating Pressure-Cover

Clear communication is critical in the execution of the coffin corner. As the ball goes wide, the outside back must rely on the center back for information. If the center back won't be joining the party, she simply shouts, "Just you!" or "You're on your own!" If, on the other hand, the outside back hears, "Force her wide," she knows that the center back is there providing cover. At that point, the center back should be talking to the outside back throughout the entire engagement.

Once the outside back had the attacker pinned wide, our center back would start shouting, "Bring her to me! Bring her to me!" This is important.

Besides conveying information, communication is intimidation. The attacker can see she's locked into a 1v2 and that means she has the beginning of a problem. When she hears the supporting defender shouting, "Bring her to me," she's got a bigger problem. That's not the sound of someone passing along information; it's the sound of someone licking her chops as she gets ready for the kill. Nobody's composure is improved upon hearing that they're headed for a death-trap. And that's exactly why we did it.

Communication is intimidation. The more you present an organized front, the more the attacker will reconsider her options. The more variables you give the attacker to process, the more difficulty she will have in the decision-making process. Don't let the attacker call the shots just because she's the one with the ball. Give her something to think about. Better yet, give her something to fear.

This process wasn't merely effective; it was also fun. Our defenders enjoyed taking opponents into the coffin corner. They enjoyed the teamwork involved; they enjoyed the intimidation; and they enjoyed the slaughter.

And because they learned to do it so well, Amie dubbed them the Queens of Cover.

28

Pressure-Cover Probs

Whether it's occurring on the wings or in the middle, the covering defender (a.k.a. the second defender) has two responsibilities. The first is to cut off a penetrating pass between her and the first defender. This is a split pass and it's very dangerous and we'll discuss it more in the next unit. The second defender's other job is to cover for the first defender in case she gets beat on the dribble. These duties never go away, even as the center back moves to engage an attacker in the coffin corner.

Here are the most common problems you'll run into when coaching the coffin corner:

- The center back gets too wide too soon – If the center back slides out of the middle too early, it will open up a dangerous passing seam into a center forward.
- The center back gets too close to the first defender before the attacker takes her big vertical touch – If the center back crowds the outside back, one big touch will beat the both of them.

- The center back is too far away from the outside back – If the outside back gets beat on the dribble, the center back isn't close enough to immediately tackle. Instead of facing a 1v2, the attacker faces a 1v1 and then another 1v1. Also, if the center back is too deep when the attacker takes her vertical touch, a crossing seam will be available between the two defenders.

The ideal starting distance between the first and second defenders is about 5-6 yards. As the attacker begins to advance and the first defender retreats, the second defender allows that distance to shrink.

29

Pressure-Cover
Training Exercises

1 *v2 Grid* – In this drill, the grid is roughly 20 x 10 yards. The attacker starts at
one end of the grid. Two defenders start with the ball at the other end. There
is a mini-goal on one corner of the defenders' end-line. A defender serves the ball
to the attacker. The other defender jumps up to pressure the ball, assuming the
role of the first defender. Her partner becomes the covering defender. The attacker scores by either dribbling over the end-line or passing into the mini-goal.

As the first defender advances to pressure the ball, her job is to force the
attacker to the side of the grid opposite the mini-goal and, this is the important
part, to keep her to that side! Her job is to force the attacker up the sideline so
that the covering defender can come across to create the 1v2.

The second defender should be communicating to her partner, saying things
like, "Keep her right!" and "Bring her to me!" This type of communication is
critical for the coffin corner to work.

It's important that the attacker has two ways to score. I used to do this exercise without the mini-goal but found that the covering defender was cheating too much or too early or both. The mini-goal forces the covering defender to protect the interior seam as she moves to support. Scoring on the dribble forces the second defender to engage when the attacker penetrates.

The Most Common Mistakes:

- The first defender will retreat too much and the attacker will be able to go sideways across the grid. The defender's front foot is the fence that seals off the ball. The first defender has to be willing to let the ball get past her front foot. In other words, if the attacker took a square touch toward the middle, the ball should hit the defender's front foot.

   As the first defender confronts the ball, she will hit the brakes about four yards from the attacker. As the attacker advances, the first defender will build up some momentum with a shuffling retreat. That's fine, but she should retreat slower than the attacker advances. She should *absorb* the attacker's dribble. If she always maintains the same distance between the ball and her front foot, the ball will never get even with her front foot and she'll never seal off the middle. She needs to dare that attacker into a footrace.

   This is a nerve-wracking experience for the first defender because she is putting herself at a disadvantage for a footrace down the line. That's why she has to trust that her defending partner will be there to cover for her when the attacker pushes the ball past her. The first defender must always remember that in this situation, her most important job isn't to win the ball; it's to take away the middle.
- Spacing of the Second Defender — If one touch beats both defenders on the dribble, chances are the covering defender was too tight. If the attacker passes the ball into the mini-goal, chances are the covering defender got too wide too soon.

Exercise: Pressure Cover Grid

A. One defender serves. Her partner assumes the role of first defender and advances to confront the ball. **B.** The first defender funnels the attacker wide as the second defender protects the seam to the goal. **C.** Realizing she is sealed off, the attacker takes a vertical touch and is tackled by the second defender.

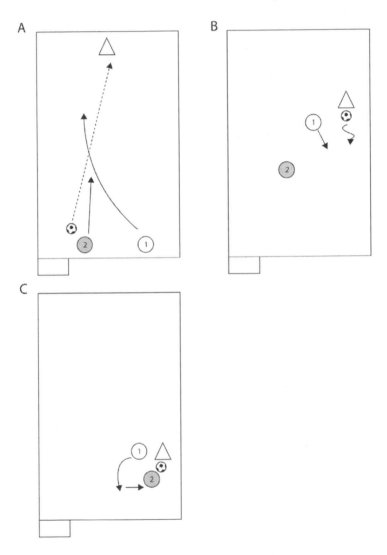

The Front Foot

A: The defender's front foot is set back from the ball, so the attacker can still cut laterally to that side. **B:** The defender has absorbed the attacker's dribble and sealed her to one side. Now the defender's front foot is even with the ball, ensuring the attacker cannot cut to the middle without going backwards first. This makes the attacker more predictable.

A. Front Foot Bad

B. Front Foot Good

30

1v2 Cross-Blocking

A s the center back slides wide to create the 1v2, the attacker will often look to get off a cross. In this situation it is important that the two defenders aren't on the same horizontal line. We don't want our center back hiding behind our outside back. If both players occupy the same horizontal line, then two players are doing the same job and one of them is being wasted. As the first defender should be using her cross-blocking techniques we covered earlier, it's up to the covering defender to fill a different crossing window. To simplify, the covering defender should be about a yard deeper than the pressuring defender. The objective is to form the biggest possible cross-blocking wall.

1v2 Cross-Blocking Lines

A: Both defenders are on the same horizontal line. This is bad positioning by the center back.

B: The defenders are correctly positioned on different lines.

A. Bad Cross-Blocking Lines

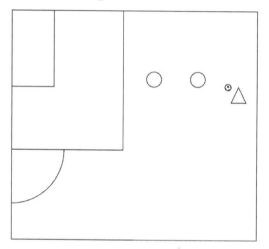

B. Good Cross-Blocking Lines

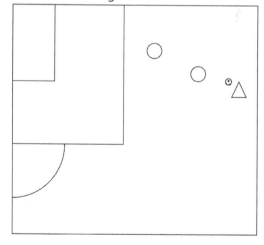

31

1v2 Deep Corner Defending

U ntil now, the covering defender has always been the deeper of the two defenders. There will be times when the attacker takes the ball so deep into the corner that the defenders should flip. When the ball gets to the final yard of the field, as in, a yard off the end-line, the first defender is responsible for taking away the crossing seam. At this point, the second defender should slide up a yard. If she doesn't, then once again we have two players on the same horizontal line. In other words, we have two defenders doing the job of one. When the flip is made, the second defender's primary focus is to provide cover if the first defender is beaten on the dribble.

DEFENSIVE SHAPE
DEFENDING
AS A UNIT

32

Identifying the Point

N ow we are incorporating all of our defenders into a cohesive unit working under the umbrella of our principles with the objective of preventing the ball from winding up in our net.

As we go through this section, we're specifically going to be addressing situations where the attacking player on the ball has gotten behind our midfield and it is solely up to the zonal back four to deal with the threat. Remember, our goal is to funnel the ball to the wide areas of the field. To that end, we must prevent the ball from penetrating between defenders.

The first step when confronting an attack is to designate the defender who will confront the ball. We refer to this player as the point.

Identifying the proper point player is a critical element to successful group defending. Often times, particularly when the attack is launched from a wide position, the wrong player will take up the point and your team is already off to a bad start. In the 2v1 Defending unit, we discussed *The Great Mistake* where an outside back steps to the front of a 2v1 to confront the ball. This is a common byproduct of choosing the wrong point player.

So who should be the point player? Well, that's going to change depending on where the attack originates and the angle of the attack by the opponent dribbling the ball. By and large, the point player should be the defender in the best position to confront the dribble and steer the attack to a less dangerous position.

In the following diagrams, the flat back four retreats in to its shape. The right center back emerges as the point and her teammates fall into shape behind her. Notice that the outside backs are angling their retreating runs toward the center of the park. This is to clog the interior passing seams to prevent a split pass, thus forcing the attack to a wider position.

Identifying the Point

A: An attacker with the ball runs at a flat back four. With runners in advance of the ball, the defenders immediately retreat and pinch to protect the space behind them. **B:** The right center back emerges as the point while her teammates are working to take up a proper shape behind her. Because the attacker is still outside of shooting range, the defenders continue to retreat and consolidate.

A. Point 1

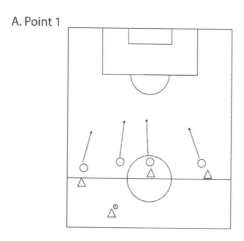

B. Point 2

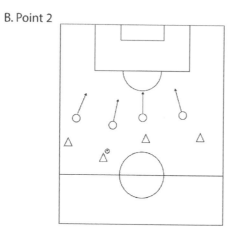

Identifying the Point (cont.)

Here the back four has gotten its shape. The point player is confronting the ball just outside of shooting range and her supporting defenders have taken up positions to clog the interior passing seams.

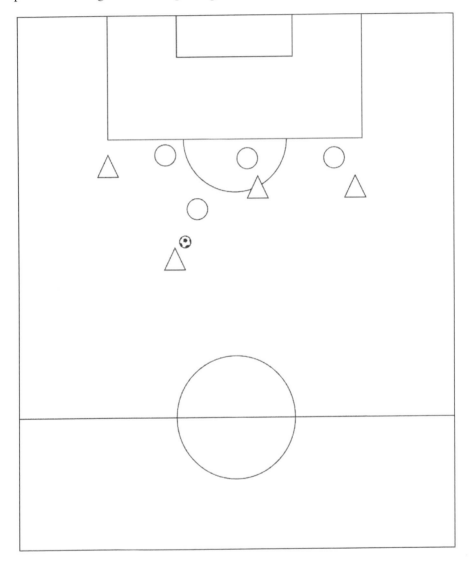

33

Point on an Attack from the Flank

If the attack originates from a wide position and the ball-carrier angles her dribble straight ahead, it's easy for the outside back to assume the point and steer play wide, as long as there isn't a wide player in advance of the ball. If that's the case, we're right back to our 2v1 and we want to avoid that. Instead of stepping to the ball, the outside back should just drop in and allow her center back to assume the role of point.

Similarly, if the ball-carrier starts out wide but angles her dribble toward the middle before the outside back can seal her off, the center back should assume the point and the outside back should again drop into a covering position.

Point on Attack from Flank — 2v1

In this situation — and remember, this is the most common tactical mistake teams make — the outside back was caught in a 2v1. Instead of rushing to the front of a 2v1 to confront the ball, she has dropped in to deal with the higher attacker while the center back takes up the role of point and seals off the center. Notice that the outside back stays inside of the ball to prevent a seam pass. Here the defenders are inviting the ball-carrier to play the wide pass.

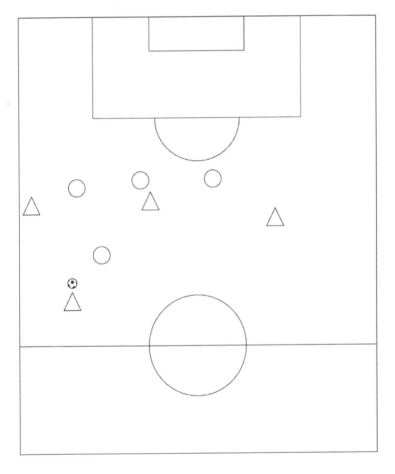

Point on Attack from Flank – Dribble Angled at Center

Realizing the ball-carrier will get to the middle before she can be sealed off, the outside back drops in to a covering position and allows the center back to assume the point.

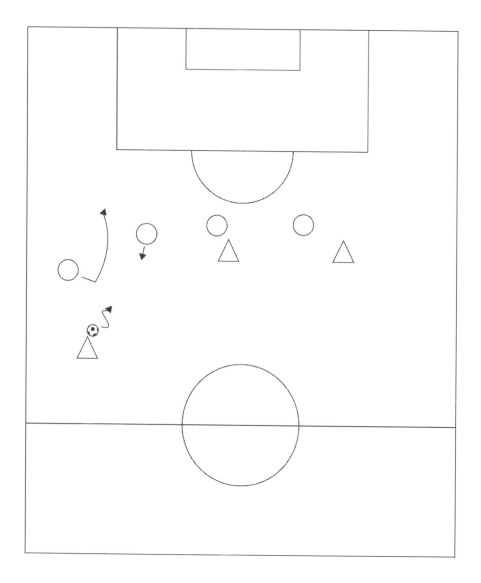

34

Run Away!

Identifying the proper point player is Step 1. Choosing the proper time to confront the ball is the other half of this equation and it is equally important.

We know we want the point to confront the ball before the attacker gets within shooting range, but we also want to delay that confrontation until the entire defense is in its best possible shape.

The role of the point player isn't merely to confront the ball; it's to set up the entire defense. When the point confronts the ball, we don't want our back four to be in a flat line, and we certainly don't want the other defenders in front of the point. Whoever assumes the point is responsible for delaying the attack so that the other defenders can get into the proper positions behind her.

Often times all four backs will be in retreat. The key is that the point player is retreating more slowly than her teammates, or in other words, that the supporting defenders retreat faster than the point. By absorbing the dribble, the point buys her teammates the time to tuck in behind her.

There will be occasions when the point player confronts the ball too late. That's an easy fix. It's just a matter of not collapsing so deep. The more common problem is the point player confronting the ball too soon, particularly when the attacking team has support in front of the ball. Again, this behavior is symptomatic of a player who prioritizes getting back the ball over protecting our goal. A smart point player will delay until her teammates have gotten organized behind her and the space between the defenders and the goalkeeper has been shrunk.

The higher up the field you confront the ball, the bigger the field you have to defend. Remember, the space in behind the defense is critical. The more room the attacking team has between the defenders and the goalkeeper, the more dangerous they can be. We don't want the point player committing too high up the field if we can avoid it. If the ball gets played behind her, she won't have the opportunity to recover in time to affect a good attack. The deeper we drop, the more we shrink the space in behind us. Eventually that space gets small enough that the goalkeeper can help protect against through-balls. Furthermore, the deeper we drop, the more time we have to shrink the interior seams and force play wide. The delayed battle favors the defending team.

Until the space behind the defense has become very limited, and until her teammates have gotten themselves organized, the point player should delay the confrontation.

35

The Seam Ball and Why We Hate It

A s we discussed earlier, the seam ball is a pass that splits two defenders. These passes are exceptionally dangerous to the defending team, so our defense must be set up to prevent them. If we don't prevent them, then the attacking team ends up with the ball behind our defense, and that's really, really bad! *How We Defend* offered this commandment:

We don't get split. Not ever. NEVER!
If you don't get split, the opponent doesn't get in behind you unless it goes over the top; it's really that simple. The natural by-product of preventing seam passes is the funneling of the ball to wider positions, which is exactly what we wanted to accomplish in the first place. Our ability to prevent seam passes and keep the opponent in front of us was a major reason our defense was so solid. It was a priority from Day One.

The key to preventing the seam ball is the positioning of the supporting defenders. A pair of flat defenders is the easiest to split. That's why our supporting defenders are staggered behind the point player. This stagger narrows the seam for any attempted split pass.

Supporting defenders must position themselves so that a pass that gets by the first defender won't also make it past the second defender. That said, we also want to be able to give ourselves as much of a head start as possible when the ball is played to a wider position, so we've got to stay tucked in only as much as necessary to clog that seam. Any more than that and our shape is too narrow. Finding that happy balance is the key to a good supporting position.

The other key to preventing the seam ball is patience. When an outside back is tucked in to cover for a center back, she's going to be anticipating a pass to the winger's feet and she's going to want to step out to that winger as quickly as possible. This is where the outside back needs to be disciplined! If she bites on a fake and starts to cheat too soon, the seam will be left unguarded. At that point the winger may make a slashing run in behind her and that defender can be beaten with a well-timed seam ball, or she may fall victim to an attacker coming across from the other side of the field. We call this the second seam and we'll discuss it in the next chapter.

The next series of diagrams illustrate good and bad examples of positioning from the supporting defender.

Seam Balls – Flat vs. Depth

A: The defenders are flat, so they are easily split.

B: The supporting defenders are deeper than the point. Even though the lateral spacing remains identical, the depth eliminates the passing seam between defenders.

A. Split 1

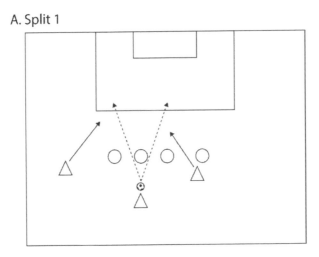

B. Split 2

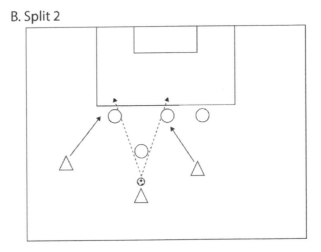

Seam Balls – Cheating vs. Perfection

A: The outside back starts cheating wide and gets split by a seam ball.

B: The defenders are in perfect shape to protect the interior seams and force play wide.

A. Split 3

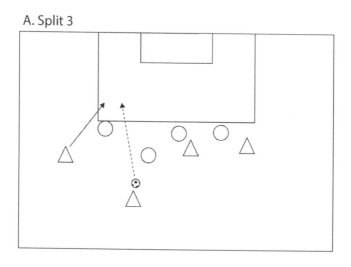

B. Split 4

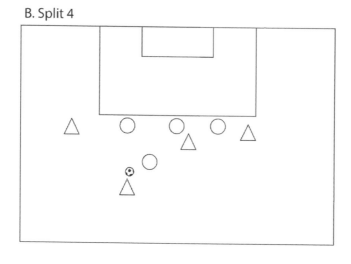

36

The Second Seam

The second seam refers to an attacker who comes from the weak side hoping to receive a seam ball. Typically this player must run through the first seam before receiving it in the second seam, thus we refer to it as the second seam.

The second seam is another reason the defenders have to be disciplined about protecting their seams and not cheating too early. In a previous diagram, the outside back cheated because she anticipated a pass out wide. She was focused on two things: the ball and the attacker in her zone. In the next diagram we see an attacker moving in from the weak-side looking for a ball in the second seam. This is a common scenario when the winger holds her ground out wide; the outside back gets so focused on the winger that she begins gravitating in that direction and never sees the runner coming across the interior. A smart defender stays disciplined in her spacing specifically to protect her seam. She keeps her head on a swivel to know what's going on in all directions at all times.

Communication is a crucial part of good team defending. Defenders can't keep secrets! In this situation, it's important that the weak-side center back alert the outside back to the runner coming her way.

The Second Seam

In this diagram, the center forward makes a slashing run into the second seam. The pass is successful because the outside back cheated to the winger which left the interior seam exposed.

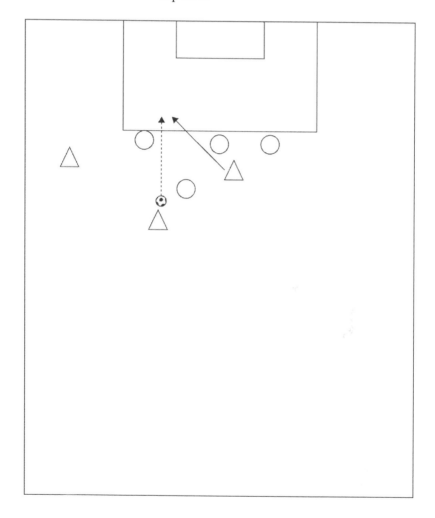

37

Exercise for Preventing the Seam Ball

2v2 Endzone Game

T his is my favorite game for pressure-cover, especially in terms of cutting out a seam pass. It is a high-intensity drill for the defenders involving a lot of short sprints. I run it for one minute, then switch out the defending pair for the next two sets. I go through this drill so each defending pair gets two turns. This is seriously hard work if the defenders are doing it properly.

The grid is 17 x 8 yards, including a two-yard endzone at one end of the grid. There is a mini-goal in the center of the opposite end. Two attackers start in the endzone. They cannot leave the endzone and the defenders may not enter it. In other words, there should be no tackling, only blocked shots.

The attackers can move freely in the endzone. They may pass the ball to one another and there is no touch restriction. The attackers score by putting the ball into the mini-goal. They have a three-pass maximum before they must shoot.

The purpose of the small endzone is to prevent the attackers from trying to play over the top of the defenders. This protects the defenders from taking a ball in the chops.

The defenders start at the halfway point of the grid with the ball. They can serve to either attacker.

The defender on the side of the ball steps up to pressure. The second defender is responsible for protecting the seam to the goal. If the attacker passes to her teammate, the other defender steps up to pressure and her partner must immediately drop in to protect the seam.

It should be noted that in this drill, the pressuring defender is always funneling the ball to her partner. In other words, she is forcing play to the middle of the grid.

The first defender's job is to front the ball and take away the outside seam to the goal. It's up to the second defender to take away the interior seam.

The defenders must be extremely quick at adjusting their positioning. There will be a constant movement of one up and one back, and that movement has to come at a sprint. If these adjustments are off by even a half-second, the defending pair will get split.

Whether in this drill or in actual games, a lot of defenders will take their first step to chase a square pass. That first step is what kills them because it opens the penetrating seam. This drill conditions defenders not to chase the ball with their first step, but to immediately protect against the most important option – a penetrating pass. The funny thing is that for the most part, the defenders only have to run up and back on a single diagonal line, but talking them into it is the challenge.

The other important part of this game is teaching defenders to prepare their bodies to retreat even as they are stepping forward to front the ball. This is a massive coaching point for this exercise! As the first defender plants to front the ball, her body weight should be prepared to immediately retreat into the role of the second defender. If she doesn't make this adjustment, she'll be too slow in the transition from first defender to second defender and again, they'll get split. When running this exercise I'll constantly have to make the point: You have to prepare your body to go backwards even when you're going forward.

The final element of this drill is courage, particularly in the role of second defender. The attackers are going to smack some balls and the second defender is going to have to square up and get in the way of a lot of those shots. Defenders have to have the courage to get in the way of any penetrating ball.

Once the attackers shoot and the shot is blocked or not blocked, the game starts over with the defenders serving from the middle of the grid. Keep a good supply of balls next to the grid, as you'll burn through them in this exercise.

Once the defenders get the hang of it, widen the grid and play this game 3v3.

Exercise: 2v2 Endzone Game

A: Starting positions for this exercise. **B:** The left-sided defender steps up to pressure the ball and take away the exterior seam. Her partner slides centrally to take away the interior seam while preparing to pressure a square pass. **C:** As the attacker plays a square pass, the first defender retreats into the role of second defender as her partner steps to pressure the ball, again taking away the exterior seam.

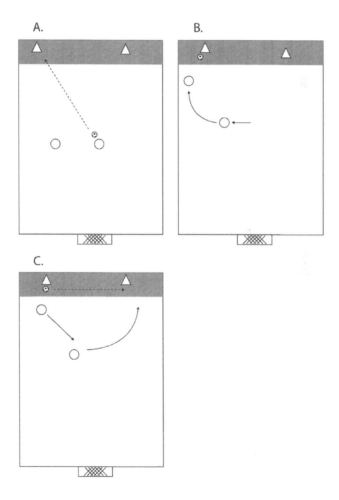

NUMBERS-DOWN
DEFENDING

38

Outgunned

Numbers are the single most important factor in soccer. The more numbers you get behind the ball, the more difficult it is for the opponent to score. It's that simple. But even as we strive to maintain a numerical advantage, there will be times when our defense will be numbers-down. This is when we are most prone. Being able to adequately deal with numbers-down situations is the hallmark of a strong defense.

These situations most often materialize from the middle third, so that's what we're going to concern ourselves with: the opponent launching an attack from midfield where we are caught numbers-down.

We've already addressed one numbers-down situation – the 2v1. Now we are talking about bigger numbers, but the principles remain the same.

Recognize You're Outnumbered – Any player should be able to look at a snapshot of the action and recognize good numbers or bad numbers. As a defender, recognizing that you're outnumbered should quickly clarify your priorities.

Account for the Most Dangerous Player – When you're outnumbered, you're going to retreat, which we'll get into in a moment. As you're retreating, immediately account for the most dangerous player. Often times, the most dangerous player won't be the ball-carrier, but her teammate who is in advance of the ball. Typically the highest attacker in a central area would be the biggest threat. Taking away any pass that puts that player in behind the defense is a good start.

Delay, Delay, Delay! — When you're outnumbered, you're outgunned. You are on the defensive! This is not the time to be the aggressor! Remember, it's the attacker's job to make something happen, not yours. The last thing in the world that you want to do is turn a 4v3 into a 3v2 or a 3v2 into a 2v1. This often happens when the defenders get too eager.

The most common mistake a defender will make, particularly a center back, is confronting the ball too high up the field. The place where you confront the ball is the place where you make the battle. There's no need to make the battle if the opponent is well outside of shooting range. It's more important to protect the space in behind the defense. You do that by retreating and stalling and giving your defensive partners a chance to get their shape behind the ball. If she can't hurt you from where she's at, there's no need to commit yourself.

When the opponent is running at you with a numerical advantage, delay! Retreat and consolidate! String out that attack for as long as humanly possible to give your teammates a chance to recover. Band together as a unit, shrink the field behind you and close the interior seams.

Divide and Conquer — Even as we delay, we want to look for moments to turn the tables in the numerical inequality of this battle. Just as we did in our 2v1, we want to look for the chance to turn this 4v3 into better numbers, like a 2v2 or even a 1v1. If you see a chance to seal off an attacker from her teammates and eliminate their numerical advantage, pounce! This will most typically involve either a pass to a wide player or a central attacker angling her dribble wide. Either way, when you see your moment to trap the attack out wide, seize it!

Damage Control — You may not be able to prevent a shot, so take the next best option and give away the worst possible shot.

Outgunned

A: The defending team is caught in a 4v3.

B: When the attacker angles her dribble wide, the center back jumps up to seal off the ball-carrier and turn the 4v3 into a 2v2 as indicated by the dashed line.

A.

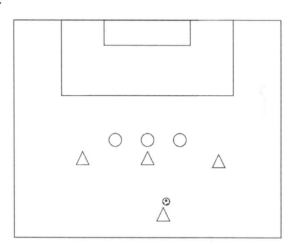

B.

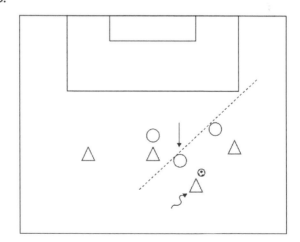

39

Passing Players On

As mentioned earlier, excellent communication is an integral part of a well-oiled defensive machine. This is especially true when the defenders are numbers-down because the problem must be solved as a group. If each defender worried about just one attacker, that would leave one attacker free. Numbers-down defending forces the defenders to defend zonally, even if they initially set up in a man-to-man system.

Defending zonally means taking away the important spaces rather than marking and running with a single attacker. We don't want our left back chasing an attacker across the center back's zone if we can possibly avoid it. When that happens, we get pulled out of our defensive shape and become vulnerable in the abandoned zone. In a perfect world we want our center backs protecting the central zones and our outside backs protecting the outside zones.

Executing this type of defense requires defenders to pass on attackers. In other words, as the right wing makes a lateral run to the inside, the left back will reach a point where she stops chasing that winger and passes her on to the center back.

Passing players on is not strictly a lateral thing. For example, if a center back is marking a center forward at midfield, and the center forward checks back toward her own goal to ask for the ball, the center back will often be able to pass that player on to a center midfielder. But since we're talking about numbers-down defending, we'll stick with the theme of passing on runners as they cross over lateral zones.

I've mentioned earlier that this book can only complement what you do on the field, and this is one topic where a book can't give you all the answers. I can't tell you exactly the right moment to release a player to your teammate, only that it's important and you need to spend time figuring it out. There will also be times when you don't have the luxury of passing on that attacker and again, I can't explain that to you here. But every decision we make begins with the idea of doing whatever we can to prevent the opponent from scoring.

40

Communication

You cannot effectively defend as a unit in a numbers-down situation without a constant stream of crisp, concise pieces of information flowing from one defender to the next. As attackers crisscross the defensive zones, it's imperative that each defender knows when to release her mark to the defender in the next zone, and it's equally important that the next defender knows that a new attacker is coming her way. This flow of information is vital and failure to provide it will cause a lot of heartaches. Never assume your teammate sees the attacker coming her way. Make sure she knows it with loud and clear communication. Remember, no secrets!

It really only takes three words to convey the message that an attacker is headed your way: *"Torri, right shoulder!"* That tells Torri that an attacker is coming from her right side and that she should take a peek that way.

Sometimes the defender in the second zone recognizes the moment before her teammate. In that case, Torri just shouts, *"Nikki, leave her!"* That tells Nikki to pass on the attacker she's chasing.

It really is that simple.

The free PDF at www.soccerpoet.com provides a very effective exercise to introduce the idea of passing players on through lateral zones.

41

The Voice

To avoid confusion in the back four, ultimately there has to be one de facto decision-maker. When four voices are talking at once, the decision-maker is the voice that overrides everyone else. By virtue of her position, this player has to be one of the center backs.

At the beginning of each season I would let all the defenders know who was in charge. At Ole Miss in 2009 it was Meredith Snow. It was an easy decision because Mer was a fantastic center back who understood what we were trying to do, and our other center back was just a freshman. I told all the defenders that Mer was the voice and what she says goes. In matters where opinions collided, Mer's opinion won out and that's all there was to it.

When the opponent is flying at you in a 5v3, you don't need a committee; you need a dictatorship. You need someone giving orders, not making requests. Predetermining your dictator will eliminate a lot of confusion when the bullets start flying.

42

Exercises for Numbers-Down Defending

2v2+2 Wingers

T he grid is 20x10 yards with a mini-goal at each end. Inside the grid there are two defenders and two attackers. There is a winger on each side of the grid. These wingers play only with the designated 'attacking' team, so this game is actually 4v2. The wingers may not enter the grid and the other players may not leave it. Each team defends one goal and attacks the other. There is no offside and any player can score.

The balls start with a server outside of the grid. The game begins when that server plays a ball into any one of the attacking players inside the grid. The object for either team is to outscore the opponent.

The attackers obviously enjoy a tremendous numerical advantage. The challenge for the defending unit is to win a game where they are outnumbered by a 2:1 ratio.

To be successful at this game, the defenders must be patient and defend first. This is a great drill to emphasize defensive priorities, as in, *When you are outnumbered, your job isn't to make things happen.* The attacking team is going to have much more possession of the ball, so this drill forces the defenders to show great patience and discipline, and to execute sound movements to always protect the goal. The idea is to wait out the attackers – to defend first and then pounce on a mistake. For the defenders, this game is an avalanche of quick adjustments and can be very physically taxing.

If the defending team scores, it will typically be the result of winning the ball and quickly shooting before the attacking team has a chance to recover its defensive shape. In other words, most of their goals will be shots from distance.

If you find that the defenders are just standing in front of their goal like goalkeepers, add a 1-2 yard arc in front of the goal that no one is allowed to enter.

Exercise: 2v2+2 Wingers

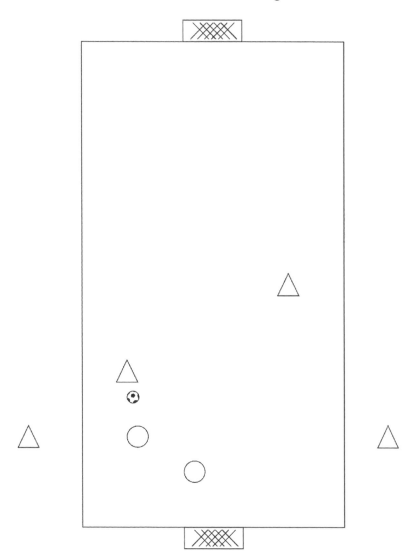

The Impossible Game

I love the Impossible Game because it incorporates so many facets of defending. It's a tremendous test of the defenders individually and as a unit. It exposes each defender's ability to make decisions on the fly and the ability of the unit to prioritize, to communicate, and to coordinate their movements. I call it the Impossible Game because the defenders aren't supposed to win. If the defenders are winning this game, you need to spend more time coaching the attackers.

The field is the 40x44 (the width of the 18 and extended out 40 yards.) Along the 18, set up five mini-goals, each about two yards wide. The defenders protect these goals. On the other end-line, set up three goals, each about four yards wide. The defenders attack these goals.

The game begins as 7v5. Set the attackers up in some type of system, such as a 2-3-2 or 3-2-3. Those seven players will play against the back four and one holding midfielder. There is no offside.

The back four starts each repetition spread out behind its end-line with the outside backs all the way in the corners. The game begins when one of the center backs serves a ball into any of the attackers at midfield. At that point, the defenders rush onto the field and play is live. The objective for the attacking team is to score. The defenders' objective is to stop them from scoring and to counter-attack if the chance presents itself.

One word of advice: If the holding midfielder runs all over the place trying to pressure the ball, she'll be dead in a matter of minutes. I always tell the holding midfielder to try and stay centrally and to focus on keeping the play to one side of the field. Ideally her role is to prevent the attacking team from switching the point of attack, or to at least make sure they have to go backwards to do so. Regardless, she's going to get tired so don't forget to periodically swap her out for some fresh legs.

Once the players get the hang of it, I'll quickly bump up the number of attackers. I like to get this game up to 9v5 which makes it easier to understand why it's called the Impossible Game.

One of the key points to this game is teaching defenders when to gamble. Let's face it; the defenders are down four players so they have to take some calculated risks. This drill provides plenty of chances for defenders to seal off the attacking group into an even-numbers or a numbers-down situation, particularly when the ball gets near the corners. When a defender has the chance to turn a 9v5 into a 2v2, she has to pounce!

This was a tremendous pride game for our defenders. It was very satisfying to see the attacking group frustrated after going scoreless for seven or eight consecutive repetitions. The challenge was massive with each repetition so every time the defenders successfully repelled an attack, their confidence grew — as did their bond. This game is soccer's version of sharing a foxhole.

Exercise: The Impossible Game

Here is the starting shape for the Impossible Game at 9v5.

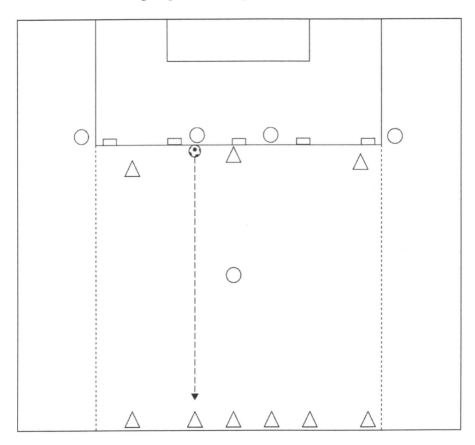

DEFENDING IN THE ATTACKING HALF

43

No Free Outs

A large percentage of goals scored during the run of play in a soccer match are the result of three or fewer passes. About half the goals scored during the run of play begin when the ball is won within 40 yards of the opponent's goal. Think about that for a moment. For all the time we spend working on possession, goals are typically the result of winning the ball in the opponent's defensive third and then immediately going to goal.

When the opponent wins possession close to their own goal, they either break pressure or they don't. Often times it's the play of our back four that determines whether or not the opponent escapes. The ability of our back four to prevent the opponent from escaping out of its defensive third is a critical element to creating goal-scoring chances. Remember when I said that the job of the defense is to give our team a chance to win? Well this is a great example of turning defense into attack. The defenders bend the branch so the attackers can pick the fruit.

In this section, we're going to discuss instances when the ball is deep in the opponent's end of the field and the opponent's forwards are on their side of the midfield stripe. Just to paint a clearer picture, let's assume the opponent is playing with three forwards.

Let's begin with a simple premise: A forward who can hold the ball with her back to pressure is a tremendous asset to her team. If she can be first to a clearance and protect the ball, her teammates will move up the field to build the attack. Therefore it stands to reason that it is in our own best interest not to allow the opposing forwards to hold the ball.

Eliminating the target forward as an option for an outlet pass is one of the most important things a defense can do. If you do this well, you'll be very difficult to beat.

We referred to our mission to prevent forwards from holding the ball as *No Free Outs*. That means that no forward should be allowed to hold or even receive the ball with her back to pressure in her own half of the field. When she checked back to the ball, our objective was to get there first.

Here are some tips to accomplish the objective.

Don't Guard the Midfield Stripe – I see this all the time, particularly at the youth level. The forwards will be ten yards into their own half of the field while the opposing defenders are anchored at midfield like they'll be electrocuted if they advance any further. When we have the opponent pinned deep in their end, we want to keep them there. Playing too loose on the forwards makes their job easy. It makes it easy for them to be first to clearances; it makes it easy for them to hold the ball and it makes it easy for them to turn the ball.

From Day One we said that in these situations, we were going to gamble. We were dead set on squishing the field from back to front. Our backs were going to be so tight on the wingers that we were going to dare teams to play over the top of us. If the outlet ball came to a checking winger, our objective was to jump the pass and be first to the ball. The same thing applied to our center backs if it was the center forward checking back. We were going to over-play the pass underneath us and invite the opponent to hit it over the target's head. If they played over the top of us, it was a deeper defender's responsibility to win the ball.

It wasn't uncommon to see one of our defenders chasing a winger back to her own 18. It didn't matter how deep that player checked, we were going with her. We weren't going to give the opponent the luxury of a short pass. To break pressure, they were going to have to go long.

Cheating – Defenders are taught to always stay goal-side because that keeps them between the player they are marking and the goal. That's pretty sound advice but sometimes we can do better. What if, instead of starting behind the checking attacker, we started beside her? Wouldn't that give us a better chance to be first to the ball? Of course it would. So let's start looking for opportunities to cheat.

When you're expecting a clearance, read the player on the ball and assess her chances of actually clearing you or even reaching you with her clearance. If you don't think her clearance can reach you in the air, then there's no point in waiting behind the attacker.

Many years ago I ran a test with my defenders. The defenders and I started 15 yards in front of the end-line. I rolled a ball toward the end-line. Each defender would have to sprint to the ball as fast as she could, spin and hit a one-touch clearance before the ball rolled out of bounds. Would you believe that 90% of those clearances never even got shoulder high? The vast majority came in at waist-height! So what's the point in standing 40 yards away from the ball when it's only going to cover 25 yards in the air?

If you can read that the player clearing the ball is going to struggle to reach her target, move from goal-side to along-side and as soon as she makes contact with the ball, jump in front of the player you're marking and try to be first to the ball.

Bait and Pounce — This is particularly relevant to outside backs. Sometimes the opponent will break pressure just in front of its 18 and look for an outlet pass to a winger. In this situation, because the ball-carrier has broken pressure, you can't afford to be as tight to your mark, but you still might be able to jump that outlet pass. If you're too tight to the mark, there's a chance you get beaten over the top. Also, you'll discourage the ball-carrier from playing to the winger's feet. So instead of taking the winger's feet away as an option, maybe we try to bait that pass instead.

Drop off the winger a few yards and make that pass into her feet look inviting. All the while, read the ball-carrier's body language. As soon as you see her body shape up to hit the pass into the winger's feet, take off and try to jump in front of that winger.

The key to doing this well is knowing how far to stand off the winger. The distance you stand off depends on how far the winger is from the ball (the farther away she is from the ball, the farther away you can be from the winger) and your own speed; you've got to know how much ground you can cover.

At Georgia we had a left back named Nikki Hill who was phenomenal at the *bait and pounce*. She did it better and more often than any player I've ever coached. Nikki loved inviting that entry pass. She would sit back and wait for just the right moment, then *BAM!*, she took off like she was shot out of a cannon! Nikki's expertise at this maneuver drove wingers batty. Many times over the course of Nikki's career, the player who started at right wing would get switched over to left wing to save her from our left back.

44

Don't Get Beat Over the Top

Even when the ball is deep in our opponent's end of the field, it's important to recognize the inherent danger of our positioning. Many dangerous attacks at our goal will begin when the ball is in the opponent's half of the field. As a matter of fact, many teams are more dangerous counter-attacking from their own half of the field than they are from building an attack in the opponent's half. A team with track-star type forwards can be particularly dangerous attacking out of its own end.

In these situations our line of defenders is pushed up to or even beyond midfield, so the space in behind our defense is maximized. Should the opponent win the ball, say 40 yards in front of its goal, then hit a well-placed serve over the top of our defenders, it could, and often does, amount to a goal-scoring opportunity.

There's only one solution to this problem: Drop!

Let's start with the truism that it is easiest for an opponent to play a dangerous long-ball when she is facing our goal and when there isn't pressure on the ball. An opponent in that situation is a big threat to play either between our defenders or over top of them. One of the most common mistakes defenders make is not recognizing this situation early enough. If they don't recognize it, they hold their ground, and when they hold their ground, the ball gets plopped in behind them. At that point, it's a foot race between the attacker and the defender, and chances are, the attacker is going to win the race.

If there isn't pressure on the ball, drop! Don't backpedal – RUN! The instant you recognize that the opponent is prepping to play forward, turn and run and extend the distance between the ball and the line of defenders. In other words, drop off so the serve can't get over the top of you. Sometimes you can't prevent the ball from getting over you, but by recognizing the situation and dropping quickly, you'll put yourself in the best possible position to win the race to that ball.

Sometimes it's a negative ball that sets up the big ball over the top. The opponent's midfielder drops the ball to her outside back who hits a one-touch bomb over our line of defenders. This is a common situation that requires an even quicker read from our defense. The defenders must recognize the situation while the drop-pass is en route and immediately retreat to prevent the big serve from going over their heads.

As you are retreating, angle your run towards the center of the park, even if that means opening up more space for the opponent's wide players. Angling your run centrally will help close interior seams. The middle is what's important. Protect the middle and adjust to the outside

We always want to defend the most important thing first. When we are pushed up to midfield, the space in behind our defense is the most important thing. If you don't drop off quickly enough, the opponent is going to exploit that space and they're going to create goals.

Incidentally, often times it will be the goalkeeper's responsibility to clean up the balls that get over the top of our defense. It's up to you to coach the goalkeeper as you see fit. I prefer a goalkeeper who is aggressive coming out her goal area. When I am fortunate enough to have a goalkeeper like this, I just tell her that if she can get to the ball first, then do it!

RISK
MANAGEMENT
IN POSSESSION

45

Don't Shoot Yourself in the Foot

The early part of the 2011 season was very frustrating because we were habitually donating goals to our opponents. In other words, our opponents weren't creating many opportunities of their own; more often than not, they were scoring on chances we gifted to them. It was a maddening time because our defensive organization and decision-making were top-notch when the opponent had the ball, but we couldn't stay out of our own darn way when we had it! Nothing drives me battier than preventable goals, and when it came to those, we were our own worst enemy.

The bottom line is that we weren't doing a good job of managing our risks. We got caught in possession; we tried outlet passes and clearances that were too risky; we coughed up our own free kick. And it seemed every time we made one of these goofs, the ball ended up in our net.

The team was in Baton Rouge and since we couldn't set up video in that particular hotel, I held our defenders meeting on the bus and showed video of our self-destructive moments. I told those defenders exactly what I'm going to tell you: *We can't expect to win when we can't stop shooting ourselves in the foot. If we're going to win, we have to make the opponent earn their goals. It's that simple.*

Yeah, I get it; no one goofs intentionally, but I believe that preventable goals are the result of players either not understanding risk management or losing their focus.

In matters of risk management, forwards have the most wiggle room; defenders and the goalkeeper have the least. The mistakes of defenders get punished so you've got to be focused on managing your risks. If you're going to give the ball away, give it away in the manner that will do you the least harm.

46

Assume She's Going to Lose It

Remember at the beginning when I said that our number one priority is that the opponent doesn't score? Well that doesn't change just because our team has the ball. If I asked any of our defenders to finish this sentence:

When one of our defenders has the ball...

She would respond:

Assume she's going to lose it.

Okay, that may not sound like the rosiest outlook on life or a tremendous confidence-builder, but I wasn't trying to produce a lack of faith; I was trying to produce a mindset of everlasting preparedness. Our job is to give our team a chance to win, and that means protecting our goal first and foremost.

Many goals begin when a defender surprises everyone by losing possession of the ball. Even when everything seemed fine and dandy, I wanted our defenders preparing for the worst. Life happens. Soccer happens. I didn't care if the player on the ball mis-trapped it or slipped or cramped up or got stung by a bee, I wanted her teammates to be in position – physically and mentally – to protect our goal in the event of an untimely mishap.

One of our steadfast rules was that the defender in possession couldn't be the one closest to the goal. In other words, the angle of support was also an angle of cover. If the right back had the ball, the right center back had to take up a supporting angle that was between the right back and the goal. If the right center back had the ball, then the left center back would drop off to position herself between the right center back and the goal. We always had to have someone deeper than the ball in the event of an emergency.

When I say *'between the right center back and the goal,'* I'm not referring to directly between the center back and the goal. I mean that the left center back would be deeper than the right center back so that if the right center back had the ball taken off her foot, the left center back had time to move directly between the attacker and the goal.

We spent a lot of time training our defenders to give quick, early and excellent passing angles. We wanted our defenders to help our team keep possession of the ball, but it was important for those players to understand that their passing angles served a dual purpose. As they were moving to support, they were also positioning to defend.

Defenders must always be in a position to protect the goal, even when their own team has the ball. If you remember your most important job – *protecting the goal* – then this should come easy.

Assume She's Going to Lose It

In the next diagram you can see the angles of support/cover when the right center back has the ball. If she loses it to the pressuring attacker, the right back and left center back can still get between the ball and the goal to defend. The left back's positioning will depend on the amount of pressure on the ball and where that pressure is coming from. The less pressure on the ball, the more the left back can get forward and wide. If she feels the ball is threatened, she'll retreat and pinch centrally.

Some coaches prefer the right back to be right up against the sideline in this situation. I believe that the right back should be two or three yards off the sideline. This gives her room to prepare the ball wide of her body to play forward.

Assume She's Going to Lose It — Angles of Support

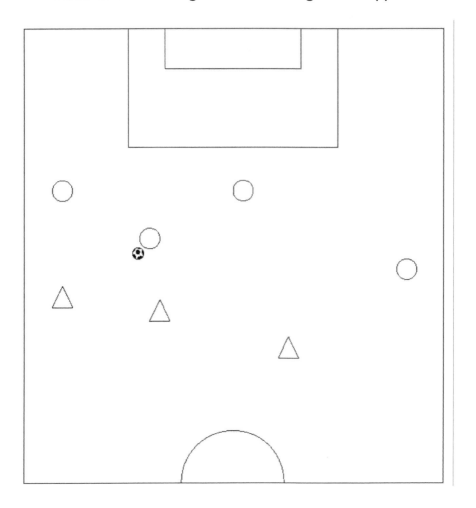

47

The Suicide Pass

H ere's the situation: You're a wide player, such as the right back, and you have the ball. You decide to play a square pass to the center back.

Your pass may get there or it may not, but understand this: You've just played the suicide pass – the riskiest pass in soccer.

All square balls between defenders are dangerous, but when the pass is played from a wider position to a more central one, the turnovers tend to be much less forgiving. One of the reasons we assume our defender is going to lose the ball is to specifically keep her defensive teammates from even asking for a square pass. A pass that is angled backwards gives the receiving teammate the best chance of getting between the ball and the goal if the pass is intercepted.

When an attacker intercepts a square pass, there's a nasty change in the numerical balance of the field. Simply put, there's a three-person swing. The two defenders are subtracted from the equation (-2) and the attacker who is now in behind both of them has been added to the equation (+1). When a three-person swing happens that suddenly, bad things happen.

Keep in mind that at the moment of possession change, the attacker is already moving and the two defenders are more likely to be stationary — particularly the one who is waiting to receive the ball. When the race starts, the defenders are immediately at a tremendous disadvantage. The outside back who made the initial pass will be caught wide of the ball and will have no real chance to recover in time to affect play. The center back's odds are only slightly better, depending on how high up the field this all took place and how fast she can run.

48

No Blind Negative Passes

Have you ever played by sound? You have the ball at your feet, your head is down, and you hear a teammate screaming for the ball so you pass it in the direction of her voice. Ever done that? Sure you have. We all have. And we've all gotten away with it. And chances are there have been times when we've also not gotten away with it.

An excellent way to start an attack for your opponent is to have one of your negative passes intercepted. The closer you play to your own goal, the more perilous these passes become. You've got to incorporate some risk management into your negative passes and here is a very simple and effective rule of thumb that I used with our defenders: *Don't play a negative pass without first looking at your target.*

It sounds simple enough, and it is, but it's exceptionally important. I didn't want our right back passing to our center back without first looking at her. And

I didn't want our center back (or anyone else) passing to our goalkeeper without first looking at her. Taking that quick look will give you all the information you need to assess your situation and determine if you should play that back-pass or find an alternative solution, even if it means kicking the ball out of bounds and conceding a throw-in.

Clever forwards are predators. They will bait defenders into dangerous passes and then pounce on them. It's like a game of hide-and-go-score. The best way to protect yourself is to take a quick look up in the direction you wish to play. If an opposing forward is lying in wait, you'll be able to negate her ability to surprise you and you'll save yourself an awful lot of heartache.

When you're passing back to your goalkeeper, there's one more great reason to take a quick look: You want to make sure that you pass the ball to her and not past her. Many own goals have been scored thanks to an errant pass intended for the 'keeper. Make sure you have some type of visual contact before you pass her that ball. Don't donate a goal to the opponent.

When that pass comes off of your foot, until it arrives at your teammate, it is *your* responsibility. Even when you feel the pressure bearing down on your back, take a quick peak before you pass the ball. If you don't, you are asking for trouble.

49

Clear the First Wave

This chapter applies to any defender who has the ball. There are times when you are going to try to play the ball up the field. It could be with a pass. It could be a clearance. It could be on the ground or in the air. It doesn't matter because this applies to all of those situations. Your pass/clearance absolutely *must go* beyond the opposition's first wave of pressure.

When you play that ball, there is usually going to be an opponent in front of you. She could be a yard in front of you. She could be ten yards in front of you. Again, it doesn't matter. No matter how far away she is from you, the ball you play must make it past her. You absolutely cannot lose the ball to that first player.

Here are three common scenarios when the opponent blocks or intercepts that pass:

1. She takes clean possession of the ball and is now in a 1v1 against you, which is a fantastic situation for attacking players.

2. She gets control of the ball and has an opportunity to play a ball in be-hind you to a running teammate.

3. The ball deflects off of her and ends up ricocheting behind you. The attacking player almost always wins this race, and when she does, she's going to have an excellent chance to be dangerous. Even if you win that race, you are now facing your own goal with pressure on your back. Either way, it's not good news for your team.

When a defender gives a ball away to the opponent's first wave, her team is almost always caught numbers down so it almost always ends up with the op-ponent's quick transition to offense. And it is almost always dangerous so you need to avoid it at all costs.

When you are that defender on the ball, leave yourself some room for error. Play your pass an extra yard wide of the opponent. If you want to play over her head, aim an extra yard or two higher. It's one thing to lose the ball; losing it to that first opponent is another matter entirely. It's just plain unacceptable.

50

The Last Player in Possession Never Gets Tackled. Never!

In the 2006 World Cup game between the U.S. and Ghana, American Claudio Reyna found himself as the last man back and the ball at his feet. Ghana's Haminu Draman nicked the ball off Reyna's foot, danced in alone on goal and tucked his shot neatly inside the far post. Ghana won 2-1.

When you are the closest field-player to your goal and you have the ball at your feet, you absolutely cannot have that ball taken off your foot by the opponent. It is one of the sacred commandments of soccer.

When you find yourself in this position, under no circumstances should you try dribbling past the opponent's forward. I don't care how good you are or how bad she may be, it's not worth the risk because if you lose the ball, your team is in big, big trouble. The opponent who dispossessed you will have a straight and unobstructed path to your goal and that's very bad news. You can't give away those opportunities and expect to win games. So don't even consider dribbling past her unless you have absolutely no other option. It's just not worth it.

Sometimes, especially as a center back, you'll find yourself with the ball at your feet and a bit of room in front of you. The nearest opponent is 15 yards away but she's slowly closing. In these moments you have to remember the rule, because that space can disappear faster than you might imagine and when it does, you've got big problems.

In this situation, forget about whether or not the forward can tackle you. That's a fine line and your coach doesn't want you walking it. My rule is this: *Don't let that forward get close enough to even threaten the ball.* Leave yourself a three-yard bubble. Play a little earlier than you might want to play, but make sure that ball is off of your foot before that opponent gets within three yards of you.

Remember, defenders are judged first and foremost by the amount of goals their team concedes. If you can contribute to an attack, swell. But that's just gravy. Remember your priorities and let them govern your decisions. I said it a few sentences ago but it's important enough to repeat: Don't let that forward get close enough to *even threaten* the ball.

51

Play to the Proper Angle

When one of our defenders had the ball, her defensive partners were coached to give that player excellent passing angles, but there were times when a supporting player couldn't get to the proper angle quickly enough. Had the player on the ball passed to her teammate, the ball would have been intercepted in a very dangerous position. In those instances, the player was instructed to pass the ball to the proper angle instead of to the teammate.

This situation is most common for center backs who win the ball and find themselves under immediate pressure. If the right center back plays directly to the right back, the ball will be picked off. So instead, she passes the ball into a safe space where the right back can go and retrieve it.

If the passing angle your teammate offers isn't good enough, don't pretend it is. Don't pass the ball along an angle that will only result in a turnover. Play the ball to a safe angle and let your teammate go get it.

Passing to the Proper Angle

Realizing that a pass directly to the right back is too risky, the center back plays the ball to a safe angle, allowing the right back to go and retrieve it.

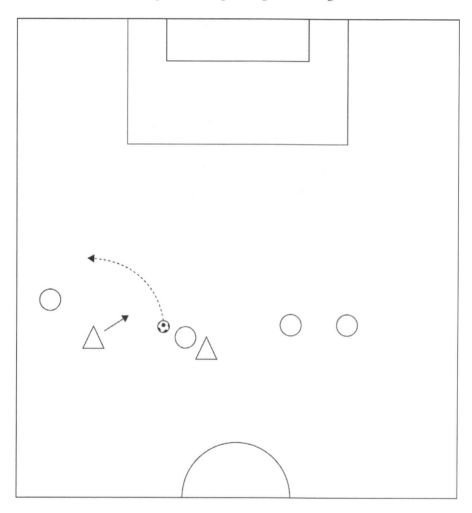

DEFENDING
SET PIECES

52

Defending a Throw-In

There are a zillion different options an opponent will have when taking a throw-in, so there's no way to set up a plan for every possible eventuality. But we can set up a plan to deal with one very common throw-in scheme.

A lot of teams will try to drag your outside back toward the ball so they can throw into the space behind her. A lot of times it works and a lot of times it's dangerous.

The only steadfast rule for our defense was that the outside back was to prevent any ball from being thrown down the line over her head. The outside back didn't mark anyone; she just picked a spot that she felt was deep enough to keep the ball from flying over her head. If an attacker posted up against her and checked back toward the thrower, the outside back didn't go with her. She passed that attacker on to a teammate.

53

Stop the Quick Restart

C lever teams will often try to restart quickly after a foul has been called. It's usually in your team's best interest to prevent this.

It won't always be a defender who has the opportunity to interrupt the opponent, but sometimes it most certainly will be. When your time comes, be ready!

The first thing you want to do is crowd the ball while taking away the attacker's best option. That's important. It may not be good enough to stand directly in front of the ball because the best option might be a square or angled pass. As you step to the ball, evaluate the situation and put yourself in the best possible position. Read the body language and eyes of the player who is looking to restart quickly. If her body is turned to her right, she's not passing straight ahead.

As you successfully deter the restart and the attacker drops away from the ball, you should slowly shuffle back toward your own goal, always keeping an eye on what's happening. If you crowd the ball for too long, you risk drawing a yellow card, but there are also times when taking a yellow card is actually your best option. You just have to read the game and make your most educated guess.

Keep in mind that if you draw a yellow card, you also stop the clock. This is an important consideration, particularly if your team is winning by one goal late in the game.

54

The Wall to Nowhere

The opponent is awarded a free kick. The ball is spotted 45 yards out from your goal. What does your team do? It puts together a four-person wall. And the only question left to ask is *Why?* The only time you need a wall of more than a single player is when the free kick is in obvious shooting range. A free kick from 45 yards away is clearly not shooting range.

Think of it this way: If the ball won't be shot, chances are it will be served. The vast majority of free kicks inside the attacking half are served into the penalty box as jump balls. The ball will fly into the box and a cluster of bodies will challenge for it. And every person you have in your wall is another person who won't be marking one of the opponents loitering inside your 18. Every player you have committed to your wall is one less player available to challenge for the entry pass or challenge for a knock down or deflection.

Some of the blame for this has to go to goalkeepers because a lot of them are just plain nuts. When the opposition gets a free kick, goalkeepers build walls like they're professional contractors. Goalkeepers are scared to death of an opponent scoring on a free kick and they think the best way to prevent that is to build a big, fat wall. But they have to be realistic. They have to be realistic about the shooter's ability and they have to be realistic about their own abilities to stop a shot from 40 yards. And if your goalkeeper is addicted to assembling unnecessary walls, then you need to command your teammates to go against her wishes. If you don't, then some of the blame is on your shoulders, too.

Our rule was that if our wall would be more than two steps out past the D, then we didn't need a wall. The top of the D is 22 yards in front of the goal. Two steps in front of that is roughly 24 yards from goal. Ten yards past that (where the ball is spotted) is 34 yards. The goalkeeper has got to be expected to save a shot from 34 yards, especially if she gets a clear look at it – which she will if there is no wall to obstruct her view.

55

Who Goes in the Wall?

I f the opponent is awarded a free kick in an area that warrants a wall, make sure you've got the right people in the wall. For the purposes of this chapter, let's just assume that all of the free kicks will be taken from within 25 yards of the end-line.

First of all, you need to determine if the restart is more likely to be a shot or a serve. I can't walk you through every possibility, and when it comes to walls, there are as many exceptions as there are rules, so let's just stick to some generalities. Typically, the more centrally the ball is spotted, the more likely that the opponent will shoot directly. The wider the ball is spotted, the more likely that you'll see a serve.

Incidentally, you also need to pay attention to whether the referee has awarded a direct or indirect free kick. Indirect kicks are more likely to become serves.

If you think the opponent is going to shoot directly, you're probably going to want your tallest players in the wall. If you think that you're more likely to see a serve, then you want to make sure your best headers *aren't* standing in the wall.

Often times your tallest players are also your best headers, and that's where this can get tricky. The opponent isn't going to announce its intentions, so you've just got to make your best educated guess as quickly as possible so you can start getting organized.

I believe that having your best headers out of the wall is more important than having your tallest players in it. I can count on one hand the number of times I've seen an opponent's direct kick hit one of my players in the head. If there is 50/50 shot or serve proposition, I want my best headers out of the wall and in front of the goal. Scoring directly from a free kick is pretty darn difficult, particularly if that kick isn't lined up centrally. I'd rather challenge the shooter to hit a great free kick and put my best headers where they can do the most good.

If the opponent puts two or more people on the ball, have one player assigned to charge the ball if it is just tapped.

56

Setting the Wall

A lot of coaches prefer that the goalkeeper line up the wall for defensive re-starts. I am not one of them.

Let me first say why I'm not a fan of the goalkeeper lining up the wall. For starters, I've seen about a half-dozen goals where the free kick was taken while the 'keeper was hugging the post and lining up the wall. Yeah, I know that a goalkeeper should make sure that the referee has told the attacking team to wait for a second whistle before she starts lining up a wall, but what *should* happen and what *does* happen can be two entirely different matters.

The other reason I don't like goalkeepers lining up the wall, and this is the only reason that you really need to know, is that way too often they just get it wrong. I've seen countless examples of goalkeeper-aligned walls that either leave room on the near post or are set so wide that three players are standing wide of the near post. Either way, it's no good. I'd rather have my goalkeeper focusing on the job of keeping the ball out of the net. So for this chapter, let's just do it my way and have a field player line up the wall.

Typically, if a field player is lining up the wall, it's not a defender. However, it's important that every player knows how to do this just in case they find themselves in this position. Defenders also need to understand this process as they often find themselves in the wall.

There are two ways that field players err when lining up a wall: They either don't know where to line up the wall, or they know where to line it up but are bad at communicating their instructions. We're going to solve both of those problems right now. So here's the recipe for lining up the wall in six easy steps.

Step 1 – Know who your near post player will be. She's the only one you actually have to lineup. Everyone else will just squeeze up against her.

Step 2 – Stand about six or seven yards behind the ball, not goal-side of it, so you can see both the ball and the goal. Technically you're supposed to be ten yards from the ball in all directions but most officials will let you steal a few yards as long as you're not interfering with the kick.

Step 3 – Start lining up your near post player. You don't need to be perfect right now. You're going to have to make adjustments once the referee sets the distance for the wall. Right now you're just trying to get the post player close to where she'll eventually be set.

Step 4 – You want to create an imaginary straight line that runs from your feet, through the ball and to the near post. Pay attention here, because this is the important part. *You want that line to run through your post player's inside shoulder.* Your job is to maneuver the near post player until her inside shoulder is on that line. This will put the frame of her body wide of the post, and that should be enough to protect against a bender into the near post.

Step 5 – Communicate clearly and concisely. Instead of waving your hand in front of your chest – because that's horribly confusing – act like a police officer directing rush hour traffic. Extend your arm out to the side and point in the direction that you want the post player to move. When you talk to her, use your most commanding voice. You only need to use two words: 'Step!' and 'Stop!' So if you want your post player to move to your right, point to your right and say, "Step! Step! Step! Stop!" If she overshoots the target spot, just point the opposite way and say, "Step," until you have her properly positioned. Once she is set, give her the thumbs-up and everyone else can stack up against her.

Step 6 – Wait! Wait until the referee is satisfied with the distance that your teammates are from the ball before you absolve yourself of your duty. If the referee pushes your wall back a single step, your post player will be misaligned and your wall will be off. Additionally, after the ball has been set, a sneaky attacker might pick up the ball to 'check it for air,' and then reset it in a different spot. If that happens, once again your wall will be off. Wait until all the dust settles before leaving your post, then go find someone to mark.

Remember, the imaginary line should run from your feet, through the ball, through the post player's inside shoulder and into the near post. If you can get that right, you've set a good wall.

Setting the Wall

Here is the proper alignment for a wall.

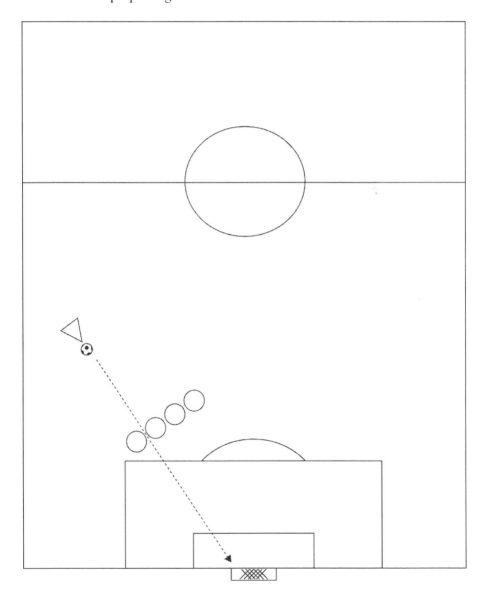

SITUATIONAL DEFENDING

57

Stepping Out of the 18

This is one of the most important and most overlooked topics in team defending. Even at the college level, I'm amazed at how bad most teams are at stepping out of their 18 after a clearance. I cannot possibly overstate how important it is to be good at this.

Let me paint a picture: The opponent serves a cross from the right wing. Your center back gets her head to it and the ball flies out of the 18 until it reaches an opponent who is 25 yards away from the goal. As soon as that ball leaves the center back's head, we want our defenders sprinting to the top of the 18. As a good rule of thumb, *when the ball goes forward, we go forward!*

Why is this important? Several reasons.

First of all, we want to get pressure on the ball and disrupt a potential shot. But there's a lot more to this one. Disrupting the shot is just the tip of the iceberg.

The lowest defender sets the offside line. If we don't step out, the offside line is set somewhere inside our 18. I've seen many instances where the lowest defender is sitting inside her six-yard box after one of these clearances. Setting the offside line so low invites forwards to camp out on the doorstep of our goal, and that's a bad thing.

As we step out toward the ball, we push the offside line higher up the field. This forces the advanced attackers to retreat because if they don't, they'll be in an offside position. This is good for two reasons:

1. If the attackers don't retreat quickly enough, they'll be called offside.
2. As the attackers retreat to stay onside, they are headed away from our goal, and that's the direction we want them running. Often times the scenario described at the start of this chapter ends up with someone plopping a ball in behind the defenders as they are stepping out. Even if the attackers manage to stay onside, which most times they don't, they almost never get to that re-entry ball. Why? Because they are running the wrong way! When the ball comes down in that space behind the defenders, it's often an easy clean-up for the goalkeeper.

   Here's an important caveat to everything I just said about stepping out: When stepping out of their own 18, defenders need to be aware of any runs coming from attackers who are starting from deeper positions. For example, as our defenders are running out of the 18, the opponent may have a midfielder running into it, and if her run is timed properly, she'll be onside. This is another good reason to quickly get pressure on the ball. The more time the opponent has on the ball, the more likely her teammates are to make one of these late-arriving runs. The more quickly we can get out to the ball, the less time the ball-carrier will have to pick out a teammate and plop a quality ball in behind our defense. These late-arriving runs can be killers because they are very difficult to identify and defend. If a defender can sniff out this well-timed run, she needs to abandon the idea of stepping out and begin retreating to pick-up the late-arriving attacker. Even as our defenders are stepping out in a frenzy, they still need to pay attention to their surroundings. The less time the ball-carrier has, the more aggressive we can be in stepping.

Another excellent reason to scoot out of the 18 is to limit your chances of being called for a penalty kick should the ball happen to hit you in the arm. Whenever you are in a shot- or cross-blocking situation, set yourself outside of the 18 if at all possible.

In the next section we'll discuss game-planning and scouting an opponent. When I did the scouting, if I saw that a team was slow to step out on clearances, it was sure to appear in the report. If the opponent's defense was going to invite us to camp out in front of the goal, I wanted to be sure our forwards took them up on it.

It's also important that you apply some common sense when stepping out of the 18. There's no point in stepping out if the clearance goes wide of the 18 and not high of it. I've seen teams clear their box when a cross came in from one side of the 18 and ended up being flicked out the other side. In essence, the line of defenders ended up being higher than the ball, which makes absolutely no sense because at that point, the ball sets the offside line. To put it a simpler way, make sure the ball is going *forward* before you start clearing your 18.

58

Defending the Overlap

I am a big fan of the overlap if for no other reason than very few players understand how to defend it. The overlap is an easy way to turn a 2v2 into a 2v1 if the defenders don't know what they're doing. This chapter will show you the most efficient and effective way for a pair of players to defend two kinds of overlaps.

The Vertical Overlap – This is when the overlapper is running straight up the field, like when a left back overlaps a left midfielder.

The Horizontal Overlap – This is when the overlapping run begins laterally, like when an attacking center mid overlaps a winger. These often begin with an attacker passing to a teammate and then simply following her pass.

Regardless of the type of overlap, we want to play 2v2, not 2v1, and that just comes down to organization. Ideally we want to have our lowest defender pick up the overlapping player. This often means that the defender who was originally confronting the ball must release to track the overlapper.

Have you ever seen a Newton's Cradle? It's one of those desktop pendulums with all the little balls hanging by strings. You pull out a ball on one end, let it go, and it bounces into the line of balls, then the ball at the other end goes flying. Do you know what I'm talking about? Well, our defensive organization is going to look a little bit like that. Ideally, the second defender jumps in to confront the ball-carrier and bumps the first defender into dealing with the overlapper.

As the first defender sees the overlap developing, she has to start preparing her body to chase the overlapper. She's about to be in a foot race against an opponent who is already moving at a high rate of speed, so she needs to put herself in the best possible position to run.

The timing of this is everything. If the first defender leaves too early, a dribbling seam will appear for the attacker and that's the last thing we want happening. If she leaves too late, she won't have time to deal with the overlapping player.

The next several diagrams provide examples of the rotations to successfully defend an overlap. Typically, the player being overlapped is either dribbling very slowly or is at a complete stop. Keep this in mind as you look at the diagrams. Also, note the recovery run of the first defender as she moves off the ball. Her run is straight back toward the end-line, not out toward the overlapper. This angle gives her the best chance of staying between the ball and the goal.

Defending the Vertical Overlap

A: The outside back confronting the ball will get help from a midfielder. The midfielder moves to confront the ball, freeing up the defender to track the overlapper.

B: The outside back confronting the ball will get help from the center back. The center back slides to confront the ball so that the outside back can track the overlapper.

A. Vertical Overlap 1

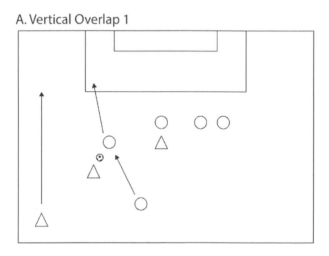

B. Vertical Overlap 2

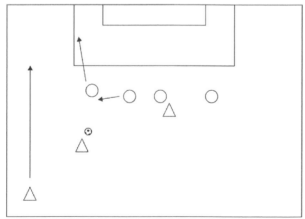

Defending the Horizontal Overlap

A: The outside back confronting the ball will get help from a midfielder. The midfielder begins by shadowing the overlapper, then moves to confront the ball, freeing up the defender to track the overlapper.

B: The outside back confronting the ball will get help from the center back. The center back slides out to confront the ball, freeing up the defender to track the overlapper.

A. Horizontal Overlap 1

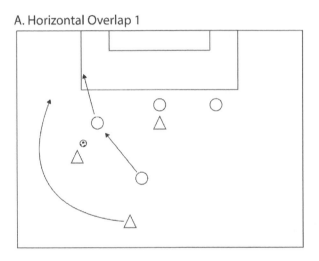

B. Horizontal Overlap 2

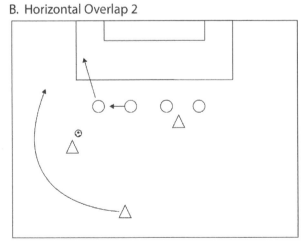

59

Defending the Wall Pass

The wall pass is the simplest combination in soccer but it remains immensely effective because almost no one knows how to defend it. Let's fix that.

Step 1 – Recognize you are in a wall-pass situation and prepare your body to run in retreat. You're about to be in a race and the finish line is behind you.

Step 2 – Don't chase the pass with your first step. This is why wall passes work. When your first step chases the pass, the seam for the return pass opens up. When you are in a wall-pass situation, remember your priorities. Remember what's important. The return pass – the pass that gets behind you – that's what's important. You've got to focus your energy on eliminating the second pass, not chasing the first one.

Step 3 – Spin away from the ball. Instead of chasing the ball with your first step, spin in the opposite direction and get your body into the running path of the attacker who is looking to receive the return pass. Now, as you run, you'll have the attacker in your back pocket and you'll be the first player to the return pass. If you do this well, many times there won't even be a return pass because the attacker on the ball will abort the mission. That's fine, too! As long as we didn't let the attacker in behind us, we did our job.

It takes a lot of discipline not to chase the first pass. It takes even more discipline to spin away from the ball because for a second or two, you won't be able to see it. It's because so few players have this discipline that wall passes work so well.

Diagram A shows a poorly defended wall pass. The defender takes her first step toward the ball and the attackers combine around her.

Diagram B shows the successful defense of a wall pass.

Defending the Wall Pass

A

B

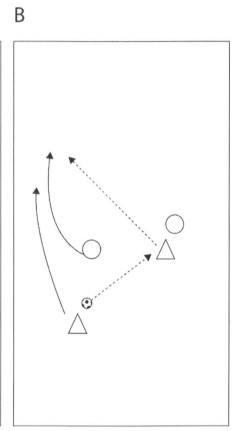

60

Marking on Crosses

When a cross arrives in the box, a defender should be matched up shoulder to shoulder with his mark. That's the objective. Still, a lot of crosses end up in the goal because the goal-scorer had too much room to operate.

As a crossing situation develops, you should be sprinting back toward your own goal to ensure that the attacker doesn't get between you and the goal to receive that cross. Most defenders are aware of this and operate accordingly. However, there also comes a point in which the defender needs to slow down and adjust his body. The most common problem with marking on crosses is the result of defenders retreating too deep – like into their six – and the ball arrives behind them and the attacker scores from eight yards.

When you are retreating into your penalty area, it isn't a race to the goal-line. There comes a point when running toward your goal is actually detrimental to your defensive duties.

Let's say that you have a three-yard head start on the attacker as you enter the 18. Remember, when the ball arrives, you want to be shoulder to shoulder with him. If the two of you never slow down, that three-yard cushion never dissipates. If you never slow down but the attacker does, or if he stops completely, that three-yard cushion actually gets bigger. As you retreat toward your goal, your objective is to be goal-side of the attacker *and* shoulder to shoulder with him when the ball arrives. The only way to accomplish this is to let the attacker catch up to you.

As you enter the 18, you should be at a sprint and facing your own goal. As you reach the penalty spot, everything changes. At that moment you should spin so you're facing your mark and switch from sprinting to backpedaling. Backpedaling slows you down and allows you to absorb and shrink the space between you and the attacker. Plus, it allows you to actually see the person you're supposed to be marking. As the cross is about to be served, you want to see two things: the player you're marking and the ball.

When the cushion evaporates, you are now shoulder to shoulder — and I literally mean your shoulders should be touching — and in position to challenge for the cross.

61

The Offside Stop

The offside trap is a very risky proposition. You need a lot of things to go right for it to work, and if one little fly lands in the ointment, you're toast. It can be extremely effective when properly employed, and that's a problem grenade in its own right. The biggest downside of a well-played offside trap is that it's insanely addictive. Once defenders figure out how to use it successfully, they quickly become dependent on it because it's a lot less work than actually defending. In short, they can get real lazy real fast. And once they are hooked, it's almost impossible to bring them back to reality. So teach it at your own risk.

I'm not going to teach you how to use an offside trap, but just because attackers run offside, that doesn't mean we should go with them. There's a difference between playing an offside trap and refusing to run with an attacker who is about to run herself into an offside position. I'll try to clarify.

An offside trap involves stepping forward to put an onside attacker into an offside position. That takes a lot of moxie, teamwork and a high soccer IQ to successfully employ. There's a difference between that and what I'm about to explain. Let's just call this the offside stop.

201

Let's say an opposing midfielder is dribbling the ball up the field. Her winger in advance of the ball is bombing straight ahead toward your goal and, as the outside back, you are running neck and neck with her. You look across the field and realize that you are now the deepest defender and you are the only reason this girl is onside and if you suddenly hit the brakes, she would be offside. So you stop. That's the stop. It's simply refusing to run with a player who is running herself into offside territory.

The offside trap is typically executed when the defenders are facing the attacking end of the field and then stepping forward. In a stop, the defenders are typically running toward their own goal and then stopping. Yes, it is a fine line, but yes, there is definitely a difference.

You can execute a stop pretty much anywhere, but it carries the same addictive properties as the offside trap. Once defenders realize they can do their job without running, that will quickly become their preference. Catching opponents offside will become their default mode of defending and it will lead to some seriously lazy habits. Having learned my lesson the hard way, I've settled on teaching a simple stop for a very specific yet fairly common scenario.

Please keep in mind that I'm not telling you what *to do*; I'm just telling you what *I do*. Feel free to take it or leave it.

In the following diagram, the attacking team has possession of the ball out on the flank. The center forward is making a diagonal run toward the corner flag with the strong-side center back, Bailey, marking her. The weak-side center back's starting position is a few steps deeper. Once the attacker passes by the first defender, she is potentially in an offside position.

Realizing the attacker is running into offside territory, Bailey hits the brakes. Because the attacker is facing the corner flag, she has no idea where the other defenders are and no idea that she has run herself offside. The funny part about this scenario is that because Bailey stopped chasing, the attacker is completely unmarked, so nine times out of ten, the player on the ball will pass to her offside teammate and that's when the whistle blows.

In spite of what you just read, this is not a two-defender project; it involves all the defenders. The first defender's job is to force play down the line, which is nice because it fits right into our defensive system.

The weak-side center back has two jobs. The first job is to recognize the situation. She has a better view than the first two defenders so she'll be the one calling the shots. She is also the defender who is setting the offside line, so as Bailey is reaching that line, the center back must evaluate if the attacker is ripe for being called offside. If that's the case, then she must tell Bailey to stop chasing. To do this, all she has to do is shout, "Bailey, STEP!" The key is to time this so Bailey is stopping right at the offside line.

At that point, it's up to Bailey to avoid running past the offside line, which is actually harder than it sounds. We're talking about a precision of timing, and it's pretty difficult to go directly from a full sprint to a complete stop. I teach the center backs that in this situation, instead of trying to stop on a dime, to break off their run and head straight toward the sideline for a step or two.

The weak-side outside back's job is the easiest of all, but because she is the farthest from the action, she is also the one most likely to screw it up. Her job is to simply stay even with, or ahead of, the weak-side center back. The stop only works if the weak-side center back sets the offside line. Because she is going to be facing the ball, the weak-side center back won't always be able to see her outside back. She has to trust that her outside back isn't collapsing beneath the offside line she is setting.

Teaching the weak-side outside back to stay even with, or ahead of, the weak-side center back is half the battle. Until she has the discipline to do that, this won't work.

I'm a fan of this maneuver because it's fairly simple to teach, it kills a lot of attacks and it's also as low-risk as an offside-inducing scheme could be. If the advancing attacker is kept onside, she is still receiving the ball while facing the corner flag, so there's a little margin of error for you to work with. Don't get me wrong, this definitely isn't fail-safe. Remember, I said *low-risk*, not *no-risk*.

The Offside Stop

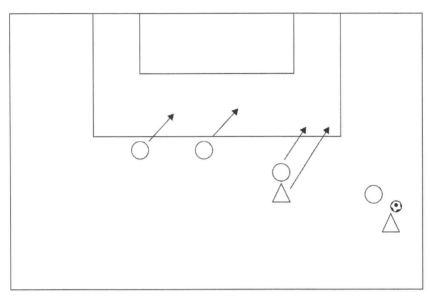

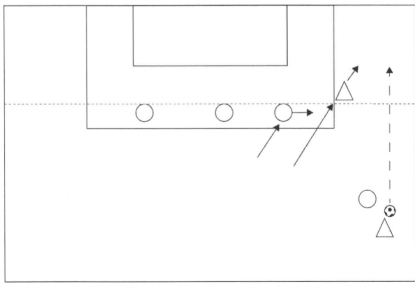

62

Shape on Punts and Flighted Balls

A mong my many pet peeves is giving up a goal because of a flick-on header from a punt, goal kick, free kick or long ball from the opponent's territory. It's an absolutely senseless way to concede a goal. If the defenders are organized, this should never happen, so let's get organized. To keep things simple, we'll just focus on punts, but the same method applies to any of the aforementioned scenarios.

Here's the situation: The goalkeeper punts the ball and it's going to come down at the edge of the center circle on our half of the field.

Our number one priority is to keep the ball in front of our line of defenders.

Step 1: The player who will challenge for the header is clearly identified by early, loud communication.

Step 2: Every other defender retreats – *at a sprint* – with the idea of being at least ten and hopefully 15 yards deeper than the first defender when contact is made with the ball. If a center back is challenging for the ball, the outside backs should angle their recovery runs centrally. If an outside back is challenging for the ball, the other three backs should be shifting in her direction.

Step 3: The moment before the ball is headed, the supporting defenders turn to face the ball.

The idea is that if the ball flicks off either player and caroms toward our goal, it won't get behind us and we will be able to play/clear the ball up the field because we are facing the proper direction.

Three simple steps will save you a lot of heartache.

63

The Secret to Heading Punts

For someone who stood six foot tall, I was an awful header of punts until I got to college. It was there that I learned the secret to heading punts. Simply put, when it comes to heading punts, your feet are the key.

When a ball is punted in their direction, most players will drift in the direction of the landing zone, craning their necks each step of the way. That's why you see so many defenders engaged in a clumsy backpedal or side-pedal before inadvertently flicking the ball back toward their own goal. Everyone watching thinks the defender misjudged the ball, but that's not always entirely accurate. If the ball deflects off the defender's head, it's not like he didn't figure out where the ball would come down; he just didn't get to that spot quickly enough.

Why do so many defenders have trouble heading punts? Because they are thinking about their heads and not their feet. If you can reverse those priorities, you'll see a remarkable improvement.

Let's take the case of an outfielder in baseball. When a fly ball is hit over his head, the outfielder is trained not to backpedal. He is trained to estimate where the ball will come down, then to turn and run to the landing spot. That means for a second or two, he's not even looking at the ball. Why? Because he'll run faster if he's not trying to see what's behind him. So he'll turn and run and then when he gets near the landing spot, he'll look up and find the ball again. Additionally, if time allows, he'll actually try to position himself a solid step behind the landing spot. Why? Because if he is accurate in his judgment of where the ball will land, he will be in a position to step forward to make the catch, and this forward movement will help propel him into his throwing motion. More importantly – and more applicable to soccer – this approach gives him a one-step margin of error in case his calculations were incorrect. If he guessed wrong, the ball is less likely to fly over his head. This doesn't just apply to balls that are hit beyond them; outfielders use this approach for any fly balls: Get to a spot a step behind where you will make the catch, and get there as quickly as possible. We need to apply this same logic to heading punts.

As a punted ball is in flight, don't drift – *RUN!* If that means that you have to take your eye off the ball for a few steps, then so be it. Get to the landing spot as quickly as you can and if time allows, position yourself a full step deeper. This gives you a one-step margin of error if your calculation was wrong and, if your calculation was right, now you have the chance to take a healthy step into your jump.

This can be an uncomfortable proposition at first. It's a little frightening to take your eye off the ball while it's in flight. But like everything else, it gets easier with practice. Remember that the key to heading isn't your head, it's your feet.

64

The Tactical Foul

Sometimes you just have to foul. There, I said it.

When you see that your team is horribly compromised and only a foul will solve the problem, then take the foul and move on with your life. The trick is taking that foul without being ejected and preferably without even being cautioned. There are three general rules that can help in that regard.

1. Foul early, preferably before the attacker has fully turned toward your goal. If you can catch her facing her own goal or going sideways as opposed to forward, you stand a better chance of staying out of the referee's book. Also, the less fully-developed the attack has become and the further the foul is away from your goal, the better your chances.

2. Be clumsy, not malicious. The goal is to stop the attack, not injure the opponent. Try to induce a clumsy, upper-body foul with some type of shove or hug.

3. Make sure the ref calls the foul! Don't do some type of half-foul where the opponent breaks free before the ref blows the whistle. You've got to convince the ref to blow his whistle to kill that attack!

Sometimes you don't have the luxury of these circumstances. Doesn't matter. If you need to foul, foul. If you have to take a lower-body foul, then play the hand you're dealt. And if you have to take a yellow card, so be it. And once every blue moon, you may need to take a red, but it's important that you understand the circumstances and consequences before you put yourself in that position. I'll give you one example.

Jenna Buckley is one of the smartest people I've met and the smartest defender I've ever coached. She is also one of the most talented. There were countless Wednesday night meetings when I paused the video to show Jenna doing something exceptionally clever. *But there was this one time...*

Jenna was one of our center backs and she was receiving a pass from our left back. The opposing center forward was chasing that pass and Jenna's first touch let her down by just a little bit. The next thing you know, the attacker had the ball and was about to fly right by Jenna. If the forward made it past Jenna, there was no one between her and the goal, so Jenna grabbed her and hung on for dear life. The referee correctly assessed a breakaway foul and Jenna was ejected from the game. The red card carried an automatic one-game suspension.

Jenna knew she was going to be ejected before she ever grabbed that player. It was just a reflex reaction to keep the other team from scoring. What Jenna hadn't done was consider the big picture.

Had we been tied or winning by a goal in the waning minutes of an important game, like an NCAA Tournament game, this might have been a good foul, red card and all. Unfortunately, this was a non-conference game, we were already winning 5-0, and we were going to face a much tougher opponent in our next match. Not a great decision and not Jenna's finest moment.

Yes, sometimes you're better off fouling. Just try to do it in a way that is the least self-destructive to you and your team and safest for your opponent.

65

Hunt Rebounds

I 'll make this very simple:

When the opponent takes a shot, hunt for rebounds!

Your goalkeeper won't hold onto everything. Rebounds account for a lot of goals in soccer. When your 'keeper makes the first save, she shouldn't have to also make a second one. It's your job to help her out when the ball pops out in front of the goal.

When the opponent shoots, expect that a rebound will appear and go looking for it. If you get there first and you're under pressure, don't worry about playing pretty soccer. Get the ball away from danger as quickly as you can. If that means knocking it over the end-line for a corner kick, then so be it. Solve the first problem first.

66

Defending
Penalty Kicks

I was coaching a second-year program at a small NAIA school and we were hosting a game against Louisiana State University (LSU) from the SEC. Naturally, we were a massive underdog. But wouldn't you know, we played our tails off that day and to everyone's surprise, with 9 minutes remaining in regulation, the score was tied 0-0. We were on the verge of pulling off one of the biggest upsets in the history of college soccer, even if the game finished as a tie. And then the unthinkable happened – LSU was awarded a penalty kick.

The referee's whistle had burst our optimistic bubble. The body language of my players was unmistakable. The dream was about to die. It was devastating.

LSU's player stepped up to take the penalty and smashed a shot that would rip the twine to our goalkeeper's right. But we had a darn good goalkeeper and she had guessed correctly. Lunging to full extension, she got a hand to the shot and kept it out of the net. But the rebound fell back in front of the goal.

On the video of that play, as our goalkeeper makes the save, you can see three of her teammates literally jumping in celebration as if they themselves had scored. The problem was that no one from our team actually bothered to crash the goal in case of a rebound. An LSU attacker was first to the ball and scored a sitter from six yards.

When your team concedes a penalty kick, the first thing you have to do is assume your goalkeeper will make the save. And if she does make a save, make sure it's the only one she has to make! You can't ask your goalkeeper to make two saves on the same penalty! Our goalkeeper's great save meant nothing because none of her teammates went hunting for rebounds.

When a penalty is called, the next five seconds are critical. Most players will switch off. The attacking team will celebrate its good fortune. The defending team will pity its bad luck. You've got to stay switched on and take advantage of this five-second window to do the best you can with the cards you've been dealt. As soon as you hear that whistle, go into damage control, and that means taking up the best positions for rebounds. Immediately claim the prime real estate – the spots where the D intersects the 18 – and don't let anyone push you off of them. Players in these two spots will have the shortest path to any rebounds left lying in front of the goal. Once you've claimed the prime positions, assume there will be a rebound and sprint toward the goal as the ball is leaving the shooter's foot.

Most penalty kicks are going to end up in the goal, but some aren't. You need to take advantage of those times when good fortune smiles down upon you. Smart players give themselves every opportunity to succeed, even against very long odds. They assume a rebound will appear and they position themselves to have the best chance of being first to it. So should you. If you're wrong, you're wrong. So what? But if you're right, you have the chance to be a hero!

At UGA we had the exact same situation occur in a 2010 preseason match. Our goalkeeper made the save while her teammates didn't put much thought or effort into hunting the rebound, which the opponent easily finished. We addressed the 'one save' concept immediately after the match. The next day at training we reviewed our positioning on defensive penalties and rehearsed it a few times against live penalties. We were whistled for three more penalties that season and didn't concede a goal on any of them, which only goes to prove that penalty kicks are not automatic and hunting rebounds is worth your time.

67

To Jump or Not to Jump

The other team has played a long, flighted ball that might go over your head. An attacker is steaming down the field, trying to get onto the end of that pass. Your choice is whether to jump and head the ball, or to turn and run toward your own goal.

This situation will often turn into a goal because of a defender who has either misjudged the flight of the ball or misjudged her own leaping ability. The ball either clears the defender on the fly or the defender inadvertently flicks it onto the pressing attacker. Either way it's bad news for the defending team.

If you can win that ball with your head, by all means you should definitely do that! Go up and head it away! However, when you make that choice, know that you're pushing your chips all in. If you decide to make your stand by going up to head the ball, you've got to be absolutely certain you can win it; because if you don't win it and the ball goes over your head, *you are toast*. By the time you stop, jump, land, and then turn and run, you'll never catch the attacker who has zoomed past you. And by the way, she'll have the ball and be speeding towards your goal.

So, if you're not certain… if there is a lingering doubt about whether you can get enough of your head to that ball, don't waste your time jumping. Instead, turn and run and try to keep your body aligned with the path of the ball. If the ball goes over your head, at least you'll have a fighting chance to win the race to it. And if you are very lucky, the ball may hit the back of your head or your neck or your back. Okay, those may not be the prettiest surface choices, but any one of them is a heckuva lot better than that ball getting over you.

68

The Goalkeeper's Ball?

We were playing a spring friendly when one of the opponent's defenders, standing just in front of her own 18, launched a booming clearance that landed behind our line of defenders. Our center back was chasing the ball back toward our own goal with an opposing forward in hot pursuit. At the same time, our goalkeeper was charging out of our 18, intending to clear the ball. There came a moment when our defender had the chance to sweep the ball to the side and eliminate the threat, but our goalkeeper screamed, *"KEEPER!,"* so the defender deferred. Well, our keeper was a little bit late to the ball and ended up kicking it directly off the forward and it promptly ricocheted into our goal from 30 yards. It was a demoralizing way to give up a goal because it was entirely our own doing.

The next day I met with all of our defenders and issued a new policy: If the goalkeeper tells you it's your ball, it's definitely your ball. And if the goalkeeper says it's her ball, *it may still be YOUR ball!*

As a defender, you are judged first and foremost by how many goals your team concedes. If you have the chance to eliminate a threat, do it. Don't worry about whether or not your goalkeeper will be upset that you didn't listen to her because that doesn't matter. Don't take a situation that you know you can control and leave it up to someone else. If you can solve the problem, solve it. Being polite is not a good enough reason to give away goals.

You will also run into this conundrum with balls served into your 18. You'll be perched underneath the serve, ready to head it away, and then the goalkeeper will scream, *"KEEPER!,"* and then you have about half a second to make a decision. Look, if you know your goalkeeper will be there in time to comfortably handle the ball, then you may want to defer. But if there is even a thread of doubt in your mind and you know you can solve the problem, just do it yourself. You don't win games by being polite.

Players tend to deify goalkeepers and will often defer as soon as the goalkeeper opens her mouth. Defenders must solve their solvable problems. You can't donate great chances to the opponent and expect to win.

69

Spot Your Targets

S mart players are always asking themselves, "What if the ball comes to me?" They ask that question even when the opponent has the ball. If the ball magically materializes at your feet, you need to know what you'll do with it.

I'm going to give you one of the differences between a good defender and a great one. Great defenders can often turn their tackles into passes. A great defender will often go in for a slide tackle and the next thing you know, the ball is at her teammate's feet 15 yards up the field. This doesn't happen by accident. It's the result of knowing what you're going to do with the ball before you have it; it's the result of seeing the big picture. The ability to turn defense into offense with one swing of your leg is a tremendous asset. This same logic can be applied to clearances.

Part of defending is absorbing heavy pressure and eliminating the threat. As much as you may want to pass your way out of everything, there will be times when you just have to clear the ball. As you're absorbing all that pressure, make sure to spot your targets that are up the field and try to put your clearances in their general vicinity so they have a fighting chance of being first to the ball.

70

The Ball Rolling Over the End-Line

There will be times when the ball is about to roll across the end-line and you know that the last player to touch the ball was the opponent. If the officials get it right, your team will be awarded a goal kick; if the officials get it wrong, it's going to be a corner.

Look, if it's obvious that the ball went off the opponent last, then by all means, let the ball roll over the end-line. However, if it was one of those bang-bang plays that the officials might have missed and you can keep the ball in play under relatively little pressure, then keep it in play. If you put all your faith in the officials to always get it right, you're going to lead a soccer life full of disappointments.

My suggestion is to control what you can control. Unless keeping the ball in play puts you at a distinct disadvantage, I recommend taking the decision out of the referee's hands. If you do decide to let it roll over the line, start campaigning for the restart before the ball even reaches the line. Help the official by shouting goal kick and pointing at your goal. If the opportunity presents itself, get the ball as soon as it crosses the end-line and pass it to your 'keeper. This will help you sell the call.

71

Physical Risk

Soccer is a collision sport. All players need to put their bodies on the line and take physical risks. As a defender, you need to exhibit an inordinate amount of courage to be good at your job. You have to be willing to go to ground to tackle; you have to be willing to block a shot; you have to be willing to challenge for headers. It's just the job you do.

There is no glory without the guts. You're going to have to do things that are going to hurt, and you'll know that they're going to hurt before you do them. Do them anyway!

When you block a powerful shot, it's going to sting real bad for about ten seconds and then you'll be fine and life will go on. If you get your nose bloodied when challenging for a header, you won't bleed forever. When one of these moments is upon you, choose courage!

And yes, sometimes you will suffer more painful injuries and some of those may actually be much more painful. Doesn't matter. As a defender, you are a soldier defending your homeland. You can't do that well if you aren't willing to face some bullets.

Don't be a punk. When the moment calls for courage, step up and be a hero, even if it hurts.

SCOUTING THE OPPONENT

72

Preparation

The more you know about an opponent, the better off you are. At least that's my theory. I served as our primary scout at Georgia and that meant it was my responsibility to dissect our opponents piece by piece and then produce a brief DVD highlighting their strengths, weaknesses and tendencies. In addition to scouting via video, we also spoke with other coaches who had recently played against our future opponents. Scouting can be quite a process, so the objective is to streamline it as much as humanly possible and to give your team the most efficient, effective and memorable report.

Here are some of the important things to remember when you are preparing for your opponent:

1. Every team is better than you think when watching them. This doesn't just apply to video; I've seen teams in person that I thought we would roll over. I was wrong.
2. Everything is subject to change. Players tend to take scouting reports as gospel. Emphasize that the information you're providing is only what you've observed during the scouting process and that if it's inaccurate,

the players just have to adjust on the fly. I learned to preface each scouting report with that disclaimer.

3. Every team has tendencies. Look for consistencies in their style and movements.

4. Every team has strengths; figure out what they are and how you can best combat them.

5. Every team has weaknesses; figure out what they are and how to best exploit them.

6. Every team has specialists. A specialist is a player with a defining quality like blazing speed, tremendous presence in the air, a cannon of a shot, etc. Identify the specialists that will cause you the most problems and make a plan to deal with them.

7. Every team has holes. Sometimes the holes are easy to spot. Other times you'll have to dig deeper. Find the players who are the weak links and figure out how to exploit them.

8. Make the fewest number of adjustments that you can get away with; sometimes that number is zero. The more adjustments you try to make, the more you're going to confuse your own players.

9. It only matters if your players remember it. Don't overload them with information. Only give them what they need to win the game. In the following chapters you're going to see that my list of scouting questions is ridiculously extensive. I don't want you to think that every bit of that information was presented to our team before each game. I only included information in the report that I felt was relevant to that specific game.

10. Remember which team you're coaching. I'm not a fan of changing your system or style just to deal with a specific opponent. I prefer to coach the heck out of my team and let the opponent adjust to us. The more time you spend worrying about your opponent, the less time you spend developing your own team. Your players will translate massive changes as a lack of your confidence in their ability. When it comes to game-planning, try to make adjustments, not overhauls.

73

Scouting Individuals

This is what I was interested in finding out about our opponent's players:

- The preferred foot of each player; which players were ambidextrous and which players were hopelessly one-footed
- The preferred foot of the left back – as this is often a right-footed player
- Which players broke pressure on their own. Typically each team has at least one player in the middle who can receive the ball under pressure and dribble her way out of it
- Who scored the goals and how
- Who got the ball to the goal-scorers
- Who lacked courage
- Who had a bad first touch
- Who was fast
- Who was slow
- Who was great in the air
- Which forwards held the ball well
- Which forwards wanted the ball to their feet

- Which forwards wanted it into space
- Which forwards were 1v1 specialists and if they preferred going to their right or left
- Who was mentally unstable (bad temper, quitter, etc.)
- The goalkeeper's preferred distribution: punt, throw or feet?
- The goalkeeper's predilection for coughing up rebounds
- The goalkeeper's courage in a crowd
- The goalkeeper's aggressiveness off her line
- The distance of the goalkeeper's distribution

74

Scouting the Defense

When scouting an opponent's defense, I primarily looked for weaknesses to exploit and opportunities to set up mismatches.

- Do they play a zone, man-to-man or combo?
- Are they well organized? If not, why?
- Can we get behind them? How?
- Who is/isn't fast?
- Do they stay tight to checking forwards or do they give them room to turn?
- Do they run into the front of 2v1s?
- Do they dive in on tackles?
- Do the center backs provide cover for the outside backs?
- Can their outside backs run with our forwards?
- Can they be pulled out of position with decoy runs?

- Do they recover well?
- Are they prepared for quick restarts?
- Do they lose their marks on crossing situations? Why?
- Who is the weakest link?

75

Scouting the Attack

As the opponent's attack will most directly impact our team's defense, I'll go into greater detail about these topics.

1. *How did they get from their defensive third to midfield?*

    I wanted to identify how the opponent tried to play out of pressure from deep in its own end. Did they try passing their way out of everything? Did they prefer playing directly into a high forward who held the ball? Did they prefer bombing it over the top?

    This information tells you how much your defenders can afford to gamble. If the opponent is going to attempt to pass its way out of everything, we can push our outside backs very high to jump on the short outlet passes. If the opponent consistently tries to target a center forward's feet, we want a center back stepping in front of her. If they are going to boom balls over the top of us, we need to drop immediately as they break pressure.

2. *How did they get from the middle third into the attacking third?*

    In my opinion, this is the most important piece of information the defenders need to know. This is where we identify the opponent's attacking tendencies. Some teams prefer seam balls and have their wingers constantly making slashing runs toward the center of the park, looking for passes that split defenders. Some teams prefer combining off a target center forward who camps in front of a center back. Some teams are more inclined to get the ball out wide to set up crossing situations. Some teams like to constantly send their outside backs forward on overlaps to create 2v1s on the flank. Some teams just want to play over the top to turn your defenders around and then try to force turnovers with high pressure. Some teams primarily attempt to play into their center forward's head to play for flick-ons. And some teams just want their forwards to go 1v1 whenever possible. Knowing how the opponent wants to create its chances gives you the opportunity to prepare your defenders for what they'll likely see when the game begins.

3. *Who were the attacking specialists and how would we deal with them?*
Most teams have one clear-cut, goal-scoring weapon. We wanted to neutralize her and make someone else beat us. That's not to say that most teams only have one good attacker. We wanted to identify any attacker who might cause us a threat with things like pace, 1v1 ability and shooting.

76

Scouting the
Big Picture

Here is some more information included in our scouting reports:

- The personnel: The name and number of each player by position
- Overall team speed
- Overall team size and heading presence
- What system(s) did they play?
- If they changed systems, what were the adjustments?
- Did they play a direct or indirect style?
- Where did the forwards confront the ball? High or low pressure?

The objective of a written scouting report is to paint a picture of the opponent so that your players know what to expect when they step onto the field. We are trying to produce a level of comfort and confidence. For example, if ten of the opponent's starters were over six feet tall, I wanted to give our players a chance to digest that reality before we got to the field.

My preference is to start big with things like the opponent's system and style of play, and then gradually get more specific. The more important we deemed a factor to be, the more we went into detail about it.

77

Scouting Set Pieces

S et pieces are often the difference in a game. Some teams barely rehearse set pieces while others set up their entire attack specifically to create set pieces. Some teams have a signature set piece such as a long throw or a free kick specialist. There are so many varieties of set pieces that I only concern myself with ones that will cause a significant threat. Below is a list of things to consider when scouting an opponent's set pieces.

Attacking Set Pieces
- Did they utilize quick restarts?
- Who were the primary targets on free kicks and corner kicks?
- Where were the landing zones for corners and free kicks?
- How many players did they send out to take a corner?
- Did they play any short corners?
- Did they run any trick plays?
- How could we counter attack off their set piece?

Defensive Set Pieces
- Are they susceptible to quick restarts?
- Does the goalkeeper line up the wall?
- Do they have any exceptional headers that we want to avoid with our service?
- How do they defend corners? Zone, man-to-man or a combination?
- Where do we want to target our corner kicks?
- If we send two to the ball on a corner, how many will they send?
- Can we drag their markers out of the space we want to attack?
- Do they sit or drop too deep on free kicks?
- Will the 'keeper come for the ball or stay on her line?

78

The Scouting Report

We produced a written scouting report and also a DVD on each opponent. The DVD was roughly 6 minutes long and usually included some slow-motion replays and freeze frames. The idea was to provide the players with a preview of what they would see when the game began. You may not have the luxury of using video but if you do, I'd highly recommend it. I can't begin to express the value of a video scout.

We usually presented both reports to the players on the evening before the game, although circumstances sometimes forced us to present on the day of the game, particularly if we were traveling. My preference is to present it a day in advance to allow the players to study and digest the information, and then to follow up with a review meeting on the morning of the game. I've found this approach to be the most effective.

The next few pages are an actual scouting report on a Top 20 opponent. I've changed the names and numbers to protect the innocent.

Scouting XYZ University

4-3-3 in attack; 4-5-1 in defense
Extremely hard working with good size
Good team speed in the attack
Slow center backs
Fairly direct in the attack; looking for early seam balls once they get near midfield
Key Attacking Players: 2, 16, 29

15

2   16

29

   9   7

5 22 24 18

00

NOTES:

Overall a very good team with not many holes. The two fastest players are #2 Jen Smith and #16 Kim Davis. #2 is the better player. Very fast with excellent change of direction. Both players are very right-footed.

#16 will try to take you 1v1 to the outside. Make sure we have cover.

#2 will fake to the outside and try to get to the middle. Be patient and wait her out. Make her go wide then keep her on her left foot! Mentally unstable and hates being hit. If you knock her down a few times, she'll unravel and get herself ejected.

CFWD #15 Lori Sunshine. Coming out of their own end, the CFWD checks deep to get the ball at her feet. We can't give them free outs. The CFWD is big but not overly fast. Gamble and beat her to the ball before she has the chance to protect it.

ACMF #29 Torri Hill – Most talented player. Very good on the dribble. Don't watch her upper body. Good shot from distance with her left foot. Force her to shoot with her right. Doesn't like contact so get physical.

When they break pressure in the middle third, wingers are making arrow-head runs and looking for seam balls. Defenders be aware of first *and* second seams.

They create a lot of chances from flick-ons (many of which originate from the GK). We need to provide great cover for the player who is challenging the ball.

They defend in a 4-5-1 and try to funnel play to the middle. They will bait passes from CB to OB and then sprint to press. Our outside backs must give deep angles in possession.

We need this game played on the ground. The center backs and DCMFs are very good in the air. Don't target the head of our center forward. If you're going to play it forward in the air, get it over top of the defenders and angle it away from the GK if at all possible. Aim for the corridors that are wide of the 18.

Angle punts and set pieces away from CBs. Look to play from our GK's hands whenever possible.

Our CMFs can't be dispossessed by a single player. We need our CMFs to be able to break pressure on their own sometimes. This team chases with a lot of conviction. If we can keep them chasing they will wear down.

GK is left-footed and plays well with her feet. Big distribution from ground. Defenders aren't shy about dropping passes back to her. Our DEFs need to step when our forwards chase these passes. Anytime a defender is facing her own goal, her first option is to play the GK. There may be chances for a forward to anticipate this back-pass and gamble to intercept one of them. The key is to take off before the defender actually plays the ball. If you can't get there first, take away GK's left foot.

Shot and cross selection is important. GK doesn't give up bad goals. If you aren't balanced, don't shoot from distance. When you cross, either target the near post or make sure the far post cross gets well over top of the GK. She'll feast on soft crosses. We don't need the ball in her hands any more than necessary.

The CBs don't provide cover for OBs 1v1. If cover comes, it's coming from the DCMFs. If you beat the OB wide it stays 1v1. If you cut to the middle, do it early or you're going to run into a big crowd.

The CBs are not quick and they aren't great 1v1 defenders. They'll bite on little shoulder fakes. Once you get past the OB, *just run by the CB.*

The left back is right footed and often gives away her passes. Look for her to telegraph her passes and pounce on them.

The OBs over-commit to wingers checking back. Great night to check early then spin out for ball in behind.

Set Pieces
Be aware of 24 as a target on set pieces and corners. Make sure she's matched up with our best available header.

Nothing tricky on corners. The target area is the top of the six.

Free kicks are lumped into the 18 looking for 24 or 9.

79

The Reveal

I'm sure you're wondering how it worked out. Well, you're in luck.

As I mentioned earlier, sometimes your scouting report will look nothing like the actual game. In this case we were fortunate that the scouting report was absolutely spot-on.

- *XYZ* was addicted to seam balls from the middle third and we cut out every one of them so they never got behind us.
- We gave great cover on flick-ons and handled almost all of them comfortably. One nearly squeaked past us but we managed to deal with it.
- #2 never got to the middle.
- #29 got off one shot. She hit it very well but it was from 35 yards and our GK made a fairly routine save.

I absolutely love when something from the scouting report shows up on the score-line, and in this game it did. This piece of advice ultimately won the game:

Once you get past the OB, just run by the CB.
In the first half our winger got behind their outside back. As the center back stepped out to confront her, our winger just blew right by her and got off a near post cross that we finished. It was the game-winning goal.

Also, I have a confession; Remember when I said that #2 was mentally unstable and hates being hit and that if you knock her down a few times, she'll unravel and get herself ejected? Okay, that wasn't actually a player from this particular opponent. It was, however, a player from a different opponent and yes, she did unravel every time we played her. I included it to demonstrate that we didn't ignore the mental part of the game when scouting opponents – and you shouldn't either.

DRILLS FOR DEFENDERS

80

Defending Drills

Way back in 1991, when I accepted my first job as a college soccer coach, I happily thought that the bulk of my days would be spent designing drills for training sessions. Well that was a big, fat misunderstanding. As it turns out, only a small fraction of a coach's time is spent planning out drills. Still, designing training exercises is one of my favorite parts of coaching, and I imagine that's the case for a lot of my coaching brethren. Your team has a problem, so you get to tinker around with ideas and eventually create the training exercises that you hope will solve that problem. You coach them through the exercises and send up some prayers that your point gets embedded in their skulls. Then you play your next match and see if you've had any impact and then one way or another, it's back to the drawing board.

When the focus is on defending, you have to provide problems for your players to solve. I don't worry about designing drills that run smoothly where the defenders are guaranteed to succeed. Games never go exactly to plan and players have to figure things out on the fly without the benefit of do-overs. I want to see every potential liability exposed on the training field so we can address it and correct it before it actually costs us something.

I'm a big fan of designing drills where the defenders are outnumbered because it forces communication, organization and big-picture decision-making. When the defenders are outnumbered, they have to commit to the principles and solve their problems as a group. These numbers-down games are excellent for developing communication amongst the defenders and for conditioning them to keep their heads on a swivel. They also force defenders into recognizing those moments when they can turn bad numbers into better ones. These are three extremely important traits if your objective is to keep the other team from scoring.

I'm also fond of drills to goal without goalkeepers. When there is no goalkeeper to protect the goal, the defenders have to train with a very high level of intensity and courage. The way I see it, if you can successfully defend an unguarded goal, you're doing something right.

This was never intended to be a drills book, but I hope you get some use out of the exercises provided and that maybe they'll inspire you to create others and to share them with the coaching community. I'll leave you with two of my favorite drills. Just a reminder… If you'd like a free PDF of more great defensive drills, please visit www.soccerpoet.com. If you'd like to contribute your own drill to that document, just email it along and I'll be happy to add it.

Exercise: Sheffield Wednesday

This game is 10v10 on a full field with no goalkeepers. Build a 12-yard arc in front of each goal. No player from either team is allowed in these arcs except to restart play. When a goal is scored, one player from the defending team goes into the goal to retrieve a ball. As soon as he dribbles or passes out of the arc, play is live. There are no corner kicks; if the ball goes over the end-line, possession goes to the defending team and play is restarted as if a goal was scored. Otherwise it's just soccer and offside is in effect (as if there were GKs).

This is one of my all-time favorite games and it serves a lot of purposes, mainly defensive organization and getting pressure on the ball. The purpose of the arc is to keep the goal unguarded which, in turn, considerably extends shooting range. Basically, all a player needs to do is float a ball over the defense and if it reaches the arc, it'll roll into the goal.

This is not just a game for defenders; this is a team defending game. It forces the players to deny turns whenever possible and to put immediate pressure on the ball when an opponent has turned. It also forces the defending team to quickly adjust and rotate when an opponent has broken pressure. In Chapter 5 we discussed the principle that getting the job done is more important than *who* gets the job done. This is probably the most important coaching point of this exercise. Players have to recognize those moments when they need to leave their mark in order to prevent a goal.

For example, in the second diagram, the center midfielder from the red team has the ball 40 yards out from goal and has just broken free from his opposing center midfielder. If he has the chance to shoot, it's an easy goal. So now the center back from the blue team must immediately rotate forward to put pressure on the ball and his defensive partners must make adjustments behind him. This is a very common scenario in this exercise and one reason I rate it as such a valuable teaching tool. It forces defenders to constantly evaluate the big picture and adjust priorities accordingly. If you just focus on marking *your* man and don't make the necessary adjustments, your team will concede a lot of goals.

When introducing this game, I would recommend walking through the situation in the diagram and some similar situations from various angles. The defenders have to constantly evaluate what's going on in front of them. They need to know what adjustments they'll be responsible for making if a battle in front of them is lost.

Sheffield Wednesday is a high-intensity game because of the urgency to protect against any and all shots. Goals can be scored from practically anywhere in the attacking half, so defensive pressure must come quickly and shot-blocking courage is critical.

You can adjust this game many ways to serve different purposes. As it is, it's a great game for teaching high pressure defending in the attacking half because forced turnovers will often be rewarded with goals.

If you want to teach a restraining line, restrict the teams from shooting until they reach midfield or the top of the center circle (or wherever you want to set that line). I've also used this game to play starters v reserves, where only one goal has the arc and the other has a goalkeeper. The reserves have the goalkeeper and the starters have the unprotected goal. You can also play any variation of this game where one team has an extra player.

Exercise: Sheffield Wednesday

Here is the field design for Sheffield Wednesday.

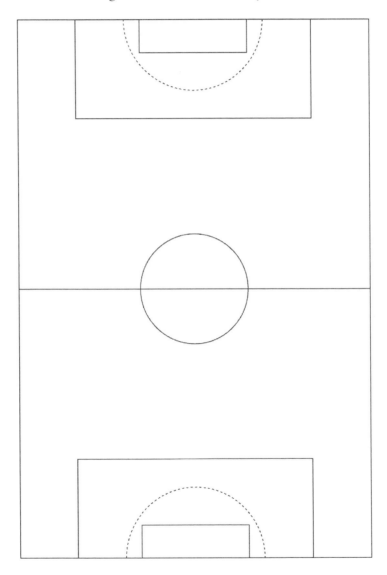

Sheffield Wednesday (cont.)

As the attacker breaks pressure in midfield, the defenders must immediately adjust to the new threat. The right center back steps up to deny a shot and put pressure on the ball. The left center back adjusts to cover for him. The outside backs squeeze centrally.

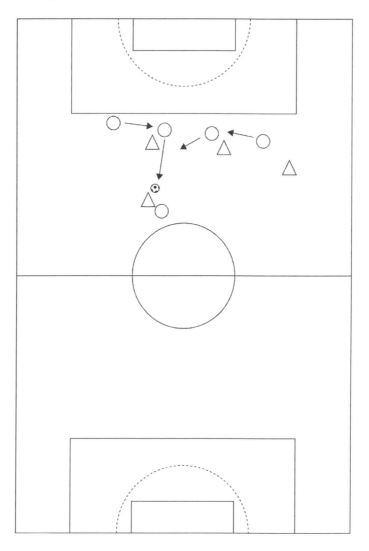

Exercise: The Numbers Game
This is a fast break game. You can make many adjustments; I'm just going to give you the most basic form.

Four attackers will attack against a back four and goalkeeper. The back four begins in a line 45 yards out in front of its goal. The defenders are widely spaced; the outside backs start five yards in from the sidelines. Pressed up against the back four are three forwards.

At midfield there are four midfielders, each with a ball. Their starting spots are numbered 1-4. When the coach calls, "One!", the attacker from line number one dribbles at the defense to begin an attack. The other midfielders do not join the attack. From there the four attacking players try to score and the defenders try to win possession of the ball and clear it.

The four attacking lines should be spread out so that the attacks come from a variety of angles.

Starting the back four so high and stretched forces the defenders to retreat and stall to slow the attack and to give the outside backs a fighting chance of recovering. In this drill, the faster the attack goes, the more likely it is to be successful, so the defenders will begin to understand why slowing the attack is a good thing. This drill is also excellent for figuring out which defender should assume the role of point.

When the defenders get comfortable, have another midfielder join the attack.

I recommend that, whenever prudent, you stand behind the backs when coaching defensive exercises, including this one. Standing behind the defense may irritate your goalkeeper, but it gives you the best view of the defenders' positioning.

Exercise: The Numbers Game

The midfielder from line 3 dribbles at the defense to begin the drill.

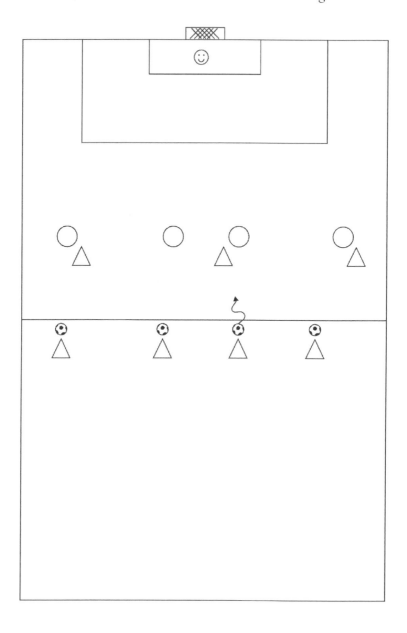

IDENTITY

81

Zeroes for Heroes

W e were winning 5-0 despite playing down a man since the 40th minute. The result was in the bank. The only question that still remained was whether or not we would extend our shutout streak to seven games.

With 12 minutes left in the match, our center back committed a foul inside the box and the referee whistled for a penalty. The defenders didn't mope – not for an instant. They did as they had been trained and quickly took up their positions on the edge of the 'D' to hunt for a rebound they desperately hoped would appear. On the referee's whistle, the opponent made her approach and struck the ball.

There was no rebound. And there was no more shutout streak. Six games, 652 minutes and 37 seconds of scoreless soccer were now a thing of the past. It wasn't an NCAA record or an SEC record or even a UGA record; but it was something noble and notable and something the defenders held onto with pride. To lose it at such a non-descript moment seemed particularly cruel.

As our team was preparing to tap off to restart the game, I saw every defender looking my way, looking for my reaction – anticipating my disappointment.

I stood from my chair, raised my hands above my head and began clapping. I would love to finish every game with a shutout, but life doesn't always give me what I want. I wasn't about to abandon those defenders just because our shutout streak had ended. They had done a fine job. Heck, at times they'd been downright heroic and I was proud of them. This was my way of acknowledging their achievement and saying a heartfelt thank you.

If you weren't a part of us, then you wouldn't understand that moment. You probably wouldn't even have noticed it. But I saw the expressions on those faces and I knew how much those zeroes had meant. The defenders weren't thinking about the five goals our team had scored, only about the one we had conceded. I was equally proud of that. I was proud that they were measuring themselves against a different standard, one that went beyond just wins and losses.

How does your defense measure itself? Do the defenders even understand that their job is to give their team a chance to win? Do they see themselves as a specialized unit? Do they take pride in that role as the supporting cast?

You can get more from your defenders once they understand their importance as a unit. Don't coach them as an afterthought. The defenders are the foundation of your team. Make sure they know it. Make sure they understand that a team's pride comes from its ability to protect its own house. Give them an identity. Develop them as a team within the team. Set high expectations and coach them to reach those expectations. And when they deliver a lockdown performance, don't let it go unnoticed. Make sure to mention their contribution. Let everyone know that the defenders are a valued part of the team. And maybe, if the spirit moves you, consider joining them for a few slices of Shutout Pizza.

A FINAL WORD

T hank you for reading *Shutout Pizza*. I hope this book has helped broaden your understanding of defending and inspired some ideas for how to train your defenders. If you enjoyed *Shutout Pizza*, I hope you'll take a moment to leave me a five-star review on Amazon. It will take you less than a minute and it's like dropping a fiver in my tip jar.

As I said at the outset, not every coach will agree with each of my philosophies. That's fine. This is merely how I ran the defenders at Ole Miss and Georgia; I'm not saying that it's definitely right for you or your team.

If you'd like more defensive drills, download the free *Shutout Pizza* PDF at www.soccerpoet.com. Available June 1, 2015.

Coaches, if there are things you disagree with, you'll feel compelled to point them out. Awesome! Feel free to contact me through www.soccerpoet.com. I look forward to hearing and learning from opposing viewpoints.

Also, if you're a coach, please remember that this book isn't a magic wand. The information is intended to complement your coaching, not replace it.

If you would like to order this book in bulk, just send an email to coach@soccerpoet.com.

Plans are in the works for podcast videos that will help illustrate the topics in *Shutout Pizza* and several of my other books. When the first video is ready to go, I'll make the announcement on Twitter, so I hope you'll be my Twitter friend @SoccerPoet.

If you're reading this book, chances are you've also read *Soccer iQ*. There is now a *Soccer iQ* quiz available for free at www.soccerpoet.com. Feel free to print it out and make copies and see how well you/your players/teammates understood what they read.

To those coaches at the youth level, I highly recommend reading my book *Happy Feet – How to Be a Gold Star Soccer Parent*. About halfway through you'll have the urge to place a bulk order for all the soccer parents on your team... or in your league... or in the world. Stellar! Just shoot me an email at coach@soccerpoet.com and I'll give you a discount.

If you are interested in bringing me in to speak at your event or to run a camp with your team, send me an email at coach@soccerpoet.com.

Thank you to Aaron Usiskin for the diagrams, and Paul Denfeld and Rob Marino for their proofreading expertise. Thanks to Slobodan Cedic for the brilliant cover art! And thanks also to a pair of my all-time favorite people/players, Carli Shultis and Laura Eddy, who modeled for the photographs.

Finally, thank you to all the defenders it's been my honor to coach. I hope you feel that you learned something and enjoyed the experience. I appreciate all those extra hours you gave to our program. And I hope you enjoyed your Wednesday nights with Shutout Pizza.

OTHER BOOKS BY DAN BLANK

Soccer iQ Volume 1 — The Amazon #1 best-seller and an NSCAA Soccer Journal Top 5 Book of the Year. The only how-to book written specifically for soccer players. Download the free companion quiz at www.soccerpoet.com.

Soccer iQ Volume 2 — More simple and effective strategies for becoming a smarter soccer player. (All the great stuff I forgot to include in Volume 1!)

Everything Your Coach Never Told You Because You're a Girl — This is what your coaches would have said to you if you were a boy, told through the story of a small-college team that won more games than it ever had a right to win. It's a straightforward look at the qualities that define the most competitive females.

HAPPY FEET — How to Be a Gold Star Soccer Parent (Everything the Coach, the Ref and Your Kid Want You to Know) — The book that coaches want parents to read! If you want to maintain your sanity as a coach, *HAPPY FEET* is the best gift you can give a soccer parent! This book includes free companion videos to explain some of soccer's more mysterious concepts such as the advantage rule, offside, soccer systems and combination play. It also explains the most common errors that well-meaning soccer parents make without even realizing it. Prevent headaches before they start by getting soccer parents to read this book.

ROOKIE — Surviving Your Freshman Year of College Soccer — The ultimate survival guide for the rising college freshman. If your players are planning to play at the college level, give them a head start. I can't possibly explain how much easier their lives will be if they just read this book.

POSSESSION – Teaching Your Team to Keep the Darn Ball – A book for coaches of all levels who want their teams to pass the ball and pass it well. It combines a thorough explanation of possession concepts with 30 practical possession exercises to help your team develop its ability to keep the ball. Easy-to-understand diagrams help you visualize the layout and design of these exercises. More importantly, the exercises include explanations about the critical coaching points *and* the most common mistakes the players will make when playing these exercises

Coming Soon

In My Tribe – Developing a Culture of Kickass in Female Athletes – The follow-up to *Everything Your Coach Never Told You Because You're a Girl*, this book details the specific tools we employed to feed our competitive beast.

ABOUT THE AUTHOR

Dan Blank is the author of the Amazon #1 bestseller, *Soccer iQ*, and has been coaching college soccer for over twenty years. He is the first coach in Southeastern Conference history to lead the conference's best defense in consecutive years at different universities (Ole Miss 2009, Georgia 2010). He has an 'A' License from the USSF and an Advanced National Diploma from the NSCAA. You can buy his books, read his blog and get cool freebies at www.soccerpoet.com.

Made in the USA
Middletown, DE
01 September 2015